ASHAMED NO MORE

A Pastor's Journey Through Sex Addiction

T. C. RYAN

FOREWORD BY WALTER WANGERIN JR.

IVP Books

An imprint of InterVarsity Press
Downers Grove, Illinois

InterVarsity Press
P.O. Box 1400, Downers Grove, IL 60515-1426
World Wide Web: www.ivpress.com
E-mail: email@ivpress.com

InterVarsity Press® is the book-publishing division of InterVarsity Christian Fellowship/USA®,
a movement of students and faculty active on campus at hundreds of universities, colleges and
schools of nursing in the United States of America, and a member movement of the International
Fellowship of Evangelical Students. For information about local and regional activities, write Public
Relations Dept., InterVarsity Christian Fellowship/USA, 6400 Schroeder Rd., P.O. Box 7895,
Madison, WI 53707-7895, or visit the IVCF website at <www.intervarsity.org>.

Scripture quotations, unless otherwise noted, are from The Holy Bible, English Standard Version,
copyright © 2001 by Crossway Bibles, a division of Good News Publishers. Used by permission. All
rights reserved.

While all stories in this book are true, some names and identifying information in this book have
been changed to protect the privacy of the individuals involved.

Cover design: Cindy Kiple
Interior design: Beth Hagenberg
Images: man walking away: Colin Anderson/Getty Images
        ladders: © A-Digit/iStockphoto
Author photograph: Kelly Jackson Photography

ISBN 978-0-8308-3793-9

Printed in the United States of America ∞

Library of Congress Cataloging-in-Publication Data

Ryan, T. C., 1955-
Ashamed no more: a pastor's journey through sex addiction / T. C.
Ryan.
    p. cm.
Includes bibliographical references (p.   ).
ISBN 978-0-8308-3793-9 (pbk.: alk. paper)
1. Ryan, T. C., 1955- 2. Clergy—Sexual behavior. 3.
Clergy—Biography. 4. Sex addicts—Biography. 5. Sex
addicts—Religious life. 6. Sex addiction—Religious
aspects—Christianity. I. Title.
    BV4392.R93 2012
    241'.664—dc23
                                                            2012015953

| P | 20 | 19 | 18 | 17 | 16 | 15 | 14 | 13 | 12 | 11 | 10 | 9 | 8 | 7 | 6 | 5 | 4 | 3 | 2 | 1 |
| Y | 29 | 28 | 27 | 26 | 25 | 24 | 23 | 22 | 21 | 20 | 19 | 18 | 17 | 16 | 15 | 14 | 13 | 12 |

To Pam

Mo chuisle

Contents

Foreword

T. C. Ryan makes of his personal experience—as a sexual addict and as one resurrected from addiction—the "case study" of a genuinely important book.

He speaks with a bold, dead-on honesty, precisely because he has become honest with himself. He need not hide what he no longer hides from himself. And his care for those who will read this book, who well may learn from his experience, *compels* him to be truthful. If he were not, other addicts might recognize the lie (lies they tell themselves) and dismiss the value. He might be for them a brother in the addiction but a pretender in the healing. I honor Ryan for his forthrightness as much as I love him for his ascension from the addiction.

On the other hand, *Ashamed No More* will not satisfy the voyeur. He does not write steamy scenes. He writes, rather, with a penetrating accuracy about what it means to *be* a sexual addict.

He explains the causes of such addictions. But his explanations are not excuses.

He presents the behaviors of the addict—in order to disclose the walls an addict raises around his or her shame and in order to root down to the reasons of the behavior.

And he interprets the reasons not only in psychological terms but in terms profoundly theological. For the roots reach into a darkness which all of us (if *we* are bold enough) can discover in ourselves.

For Ryan, the Bible is the source both of understanding and of healing. The Bible and many other Christian resources. Where is Jesus in this drama? What is the spiritual stage upon which the drama is played out? How many acts does the drama have? How do Christian communities serve the addict who yearns to rise up and out of the morass?

The steps toward transformation: they are not merely "do this" and then "do that," and then you are there. They are not a practical sequence of admonitions, as though the addict might follow the sort of regimen a bodybuilder follows. Transformation is an organic process: soul-activity, God-communications, setbacks, anguish, moments of astonished surprise, moments of speechless gratitude, ongoing, ongoing.

Ryan opens up the whole process to those who are not addicted but who participate in the addictions of others or who would help the addict. Moreover, he involves whole communities in his study. And his theologies are of wonderful value to any Christian anywhere, since the addict's experience becomes a metaphor that illuminates significant elements of everyone's spiritual life.

I can think of no one better than Ryan to examine the broken soul: well-read, blessed with an uncommon intelligence, pastoral, compassionate, forgiven and full of forgiveness.

Walter Wangerin Jr.

Preface

I spent over forty years in a wilderness. I was a successful church planter, a good pastor and a good preacher. But those elements aren't adequate to summarize my journey. In the wilderness of wandering and struggle, of serving and shortcuts, God planted within me the desire for wholeness, for an integrated life. And as he has with so many others, God has graciously taken the broken pieces of my life and begun a miraculous work of transformation.

My particular wilderness was characterized by many things, but one dominant feature in the landscape of my struggle was compulsive sexual behavior. The fact that I was (and am) a sex addict made my journey harder and lonelier. It's very difficult and intimidating to share my story, but I offer it to help others who are dying in similar wildernesses today. And they are many.

In fact, we have an enormous problem. About ten years ago, pornography was a 57-billion-dollar, worldwide industry, and 12 billion of this amount was U.S. revenue. Now, if you're like me, big numbers like these don't mean much, because you can't relate to them. So look at it this way: The 12 billion Americans spent on porn every year was more than the combined revenues of all professional football, baseball and basketball franchises. It was more than the combined revenues of ABC, CBS and NBC.[1]

As of 2003, 2.5 billion dollars of the 12 billion Americans spent went to Internet pornography. At that time 25 percent of total search engine requests were porn-related and 12 percent of all websites were pornographic. Child pornography was generating 3 billion dollars annually, and 90 percent of 8- to 16-year-olds had viewed porn online (most of them while doing homework).[2] By the time you read these numbers, they are considerably dated, and the current reality is likely much more advanced.

These statistics are strong indicators of one particularly virulent aspect of our culture of consumerism. The questions we need to address are why we consume so many forms of sexual expression, and *what effect* our increasing appetite for sex has on us as individuals and as a society.

While some mental health experts still debate whether compulsive abuse of one's own sexuality should be classified as an addiction or not, and while late-night comedians continue to make fun of the public figures who are caught in the struggle with their compulsive sexual behavior, the onslaught of America continues. The father of sex-addiction research, Patrick Carnes, estimated years ago that 6 to 10 percent of the U.S. adult population was sexually addicted. It's clear that today that number is more around 40 percent.[3] That is a huge, huge number. We are facing a debilitating social epidemic. And a domain once believed to belong to males has clearly become occupied by both men and women. Internet pornography is a significant factor in causing increasing numbers of women to struggle with sexual addiction.

One might hope that those who are working on their spirituality—those in the church, for instance—are faring better than the rest at handling such a difficult challenge. Tragically, that is not the case. For instance, one study revealed that 53 percent of Promise Keepers men (men attending rallies and meetings to help them develop healthy male spirituality and devotion) admitted to viewing pornography the previous week.[4] In her remarkable book, *No Stones,* author Marnie Ferree pulled back the shroud over women afflicted by sex addiction. She cites a 2006 poll in which 20 percent of Christian women reported an addiction to porn.[5]

One of the increasingly debilitating behaviors in this technologically driven age is the use of chat rooms. Ferree tells us that of the many women who move from viewing Internet pornography to visiting chat rooms, many of them develop cyber relationships online and almost 80 percent of women in sex-oriented chat rooms go on to meet their chat partners.[6] We have an enormous problem, and we don't seem to know what to do about it.

As a man who has struggles with lust and pornography, I want to apologize to women in general and specifically to all the women in my life. Porn and lust and compulsive behaviors give lie to the powerful reality that women are created in the image of God, bearing the Creator's qualities of nurture and vulnerability, beauty and maternal warmth, intelligence and connection. As sexual brokenness comes as a result of intimacy impairment, so often our acting out is a result of longing for the intangibles which sex can never meet, but deep down we intuitively understand that we long for.

The next generation is under siege. Today a nine-year-old boy will receive an email image on his own cell phone that contains images of men and women sexually abusing each other. He will not know how to process it, but will receive the message that "this is what adults do; this is what sex is." Today an eleven-year-old girl will perform a sexual act on an older boy because she is being taught in this culture that her value exists in using her person and sexuality to service others. These are not extreme examples; they are ordinary. They are happening many times every day.

I don't pretend to have all the answers for what we need to do. Nor is it my place to reform the church in the area of sexual brokenness. But I have a story, and it's more about God and who he is than about me, and it's more about hope when there is no hope than it is about me. It's about grace and the power of God to reach and change a life when there is no human hope that such a thing is possible.

I'm sharing my story—and the thoughts I have because of it—to encourage those who are facing huge personal challenges and are losing hope. Some of you who read these words may be older, like me, and so worn by the struggle that you're close to giving up. Some of you who are younger aren't so worn down or afraid, but you're beginning to sense that you're in deep trouble. Some of you are in professional ministry or are preparing for it, and the dichotomy of your call and your compulsion are eating away at you.

If you match any of those descriptions, you are struggling with a hidden self and with shame—like I did for so long—and you don't know what to do. I'm writing to say that there is real hope in the midst of real struggle. Sometimes it doesn't come around very fast. Often, when it does come around, we're not open to it. But still there is hope for all of us. If you find your life is difficult, you're not alone. And you won't always be where it seems you are right now.

There are others I hope benefit from these words of mine. Some of you have friends or family in trouble with compulsive behaviors, and you don't know what to do. Those of us who make up the church are firmly in that group whether we know it or not. I am also writing for those who are responsible for our seminaries, Bible schools and the institutions which govern and direct the church and her ministries. I hope my experiences and observations are useful to you as you offer guidance and care for others.

I am a man who has throughout most of his adult life made bad choices, persisted in bad behaviors and cultivated bad patterns. These all resulted in bad consequences that I worked hard to deserve. But in spite of my brokenness and stubbornness, God has been tenaciously kind to me. Because of the love and pitying mercy of God and the unflagging support of my spouse and closest friends, I am today a humbled man who more often than not makes good choices, repeats good behaviors and is cultivating good patterns of living.

Some months after I left both the ministry and the church my wife and I had planted nineteen years earlier, I was deep into the most intensive psychotherapy I could imagine. My soul was bare and my feelings were raw. I spent part of one day lying on the floor, trying to remember what my name was. Early one morning I was sitting in our study, a lit votive candle before me illuminating an icon of Christ. After my opening prayers, I began to read the daily texts from the *St. James Daily Devotional Guide for the Christian Year,* one of which was Luke 22. The words of verse 31 came off the page. My eyes locked on the letters, and I felt the Holy Spirit telling me to pay special attention to them.

> Simon, Simon, Satan has asked to sift you as wheat.
> But I have prayed for you, Simon, that your faith may
>   not fail.
> And when you have turned back, strengthen your brothers.
>   (NIV 1984)

Ashamed No More is a part of my effort to be obedient to that word. In the sifting that has been part of my life, I have been found to be terribly broken—and wildly loved. I write for my brothers and sisters who are suffering greatly today, for those suffering with them and for those who would make the church a safer place for honest strugglers. God will not waste our pain if we cooperate with him.

Living a Divided Life

Come to me, all who labor and are heavy laden, and I will give you rest.
Take my yoke upon you, and learn from me, for I am gentle
and lowly in heart, and you will find rest for your souls.
For my yoke is easy, and my burden is light.

—JESUS OF NAZARETH (MATTHEW 11:28-30)

I was sitting on the trunk of a fallen tree beside a creek, and I was miserable. I was aware we were having one of those warm, sun-splashed days that make spring so sweet, yet I wasn't feeling anything but dullness, despair and self-loathing. Hopelessness was suffocating me.

I was in a park, getting porn. For sixteen years I had worked at recovering from compulsive sexual behaviors, and there I was—after nine years of therapy, years of groups and sponsors, a lot of work and struggle—and I was getting porn. For years, I'd had porn blocked on my laptop. Yet there I was, getting porn in a park. I was so down I didn't see any way of going on, going back or getting out. I saw no way.

I turned my face toward the blue sky and prayed, "God in heaven, I cannot believe after everything I've done and all the grace you've shown me, I'm here in this place, just cycling and cycling and cycling. I can't stand this life anymore. I don't care what you want from me—anything, anything—but I can't stand this life anymore. I don't care what you do with me, but you have to do something. Please."

I had not lost my faith. But I had lost hope. I was hopelessly stuck.

■ ■ ■

Life is difficult. Living life well is hard. Don't let anyone tell you otherwise. Life may seem more challenging for some than for others, but all of us have challenges that make life complicated.

I am not writing to celebrate my struggle or hold myself up as a unique victim of cruel circumstances. Neither is it my intention to blame others for my difficulties. My story is no more unique or special than anyone else's. But it is worth sharing because for a long, long time I lived without hope, and now I have hope.

For more than forty years, a defining and crippling characteristic of my life was a daily struggle with compulsive sexual behavior. I was a dopamine and adrenaline junky. I used my sexuality to get my "drugs." But my problem wasn't just sex. Anyone who is an addict and then experiences genuine recovery from addiction sooner or later learns that addictions are not our real problem. Addictions or compulsive behaviors are merely the symptoms of something deeper.

My life was hard and chaotic. I was gifted and I was loved. I was angry and I was moody. I despaired and I was depressed. I was impulsive and compulsive. I was effective and successful, and I was a mess. Sometimes I even made it harder and more chaotic, though I usually didn't see it that way at the time. I was trapped, and try as I might, I had a prolonged struggle to find my way out of the wilderness of compulsive behavior and chaotic living.

For the longest time—roughly the first twenty-five years of my forty-year sojourn in the wilderness of chaotic living—I was firmly committed to solving my problems *on my own*. That doesn't mean I was the only one aware of my problems, just that I was a determined isolationist. I came by that honestly, as do a lot of us. It's an odd thing, I suppose, or maybe it's really not odd at all, that most of us who've been really hurt or disappointed are very careful whom we share ourselves with, and we never tell our secrets to other people. We're convinced some parts of life are meant to be handled within the deep walls of protective loneliness, and we believe that to try any other approach would surely bring more hurt and more shame. I was one of those people.

The Fascinating Dynamic of Shadow

We all have a notion of who we are, what we like, what our best characteristics are, the face we show others. But behind our persona, often below the level of self-awareness, is our shadow—that part of ourselves we don't like. A lot of our energy can go into ignoring, denying or hiding our shadow, both from ourselves and from others. We are better served by using that energy to come to terms with our shadow.

The easiest, quickest way to find the substance of our shadow is to think of the folks who create difficulty for us and irritate us. If we list the characteristics about them that bother us the most, we have a good picture of our own shadow.

Why is this important? Because self-awareness is essential to spiritual growth. Self-awareness and self-understanding alone are not enough, but they are required. At the heart of it, all our problems are spiritual in nature. William Miller wrote, "To know one's hidden self is to be able to do something about being in charge of it. . . . We can be our own man or our own woman only when we have come to grips with the dynamic content of our shadow."[1] So many of us struggle with our behaviors and the fallout of how our personalities create difficulties for us and for others, and we have no idea why. We live lives of perpetual frustration, maybe being defensive, too often acquiescing to others' demands, struggling with feeling like a failure. For all of us, the first step is becoming aware of who we really are. Coming to terms with our shadow is essential for us to make changes that foster personal growth and a better life.

Getting in touch with my shadow was hard. It terrified me. It was big and dark, and I really, really did not want to do it. I hadn't even addressed compulsive sexual behaviors yet. I didn't understand the elements of recovery or how the addiction cycle works, and it would be years and years before I'd experience the transformation I longed for. Just the first step of facing my shadow was daunting.

I wrote in my journal during this time that facing my shadow felt cold and dark, and that it really scared me. Did I really want to face my own darkness? Did I have what it took to face the thoughts, impulses, actions and drives that I hid from everyone else and exerted concentrated effort to minimize in my own consciousness? Did I really want the light of day to shine on the night of my shadowy existence?

What Is Sexual Addiction?

My first therapist introduced me to the concept of sexual addiction. Honestly, I do not think I had heard that term until he spoke it to me. He suggested I read a book by Patrick Carnes, *Out of the Shadows*,[2] and when I took his advice, I began the slow, difficult journey of changing the trajectory of my life.

I went to a popular bookstore in the midtown area of our city to find the book, and as I stood at the cash register to buy it, I was thinking about how, if anyone who knew me saw me there with it, I would casually dismiss it as something I was getting for helping a parishioner. Soon enough, that would be true; that parishioner was me. I devoured the book and was astonished to find so many of the aspects of my life spelled out in it. I was intrigued and a little relieved as I read about the belief system of addicts and the self-replicating cycle of addiction. Some of my life was beginning to make sense.

Sexual addiction is a person's use of sex to alter moods that progresses to the point where they are unable to control their use of sex, suffer consequences and are behaving contrary to their will and desire. The key elements are that it is progressive, creates a sense of preoccupation, becomes a substitute for healthy relating, takes over a person's will and is pathological in nature—that is, addiction is always about the destruction of human life.

Most folks who struggle with compulsive sexual behaviors do not know they're addicts, at least at first. It may be that the frame of their interpersonal behavior has always included openness to sexual experimentation. Even if that's not the case, we all have a tendency to dismiss certain activities as mistakes, errors in judgment or things we don't think are good but just aren't that big a deal.

All of us rationalize patterns that develop in our lives. To varying degrees, we all experience the frog-in-the-kettle-of-boiling-water syndrome in our behaviors and appetites. I know a number of folks with great financial resources who are living lives of comfort and excess they probably never imagined they'd be able to enjoy. And the amount of excess is so great that they've lost perspective; they've grown into the lifestyle they're in and don't see the increasingly gross disparity between their personal spending and their values. It's the same with sexual addiction for most of us. A seemingly innocuous behavior grew into a huge problem without us realizing what was going on.

In his now-classic *Addiction and Grace*, Gerald May writes that an addiction is "a state of compulsion, obsession, or preoccupation that enslaves a person's will and desire."[3] May's is a fairly open definition, one that can be applied to a wide range of behaviors, far beyond alcohol or drugs. It names each of the key components that any addict has to confront.

What does May mean that an addict is one who is in a "state" of compulsive living? The person has a lifestyle—addiction—and that has become their way of being. Most addicts can go cold turkey from their drug of choice for a time, and many often do in an attempt to prove to themselves or others that they are not an addict. But an addict always returns to the behavior. Always. It is the state of coping, the state of bypassing, the state of self-preserving.

The elements of compulsion, obsession or preoccupation are important to consider when thinking about addiction in our lives or the lives of those around us. *Compulsion* means that, however rationally absurd the motivation for a behavior is, the person finds it irresistible. And *obsession* is an unwanted feeling, idea or thought fixated in a person's consciousness to the point he simply cannot rationalize it away or avoid it. Often, obsessive thoughts come with or create a sense of anxiety that heightens their power. *Preoccupation* means the person's mind is so engrossed with the impulse or thought that she actually cannot successfully redirect her attention to anything else for any length of time.

May writes that addiction is present when the person's will

and desire are enslaved. The person is not free; he does not have the choice to act differently. It means the addict has become a slave of something else, that there is a master who is in control of the addict's life. In the eighties, a notable figure in American life proposed a campaign to cause a reduction in drug use in our society. The well-promoted phrase from the campaign was "Just Say No" (to drugs). For recreational drug users, the slogan may or may not have had some value in promoting the idea that they search for an alternative use of their time and resources. But for the drug addict, there couldn't have been a more meaningless and less effective approach. An addict cannot "just say no" to the compulsion.

An addict simply cannot "just say no" once they have crossed the line into compulsive behavior. Someone with an addictive personality needs so much more than such a simple slogan. To an addict, that slogan is appalling in its assumption and implied condemnation. It assumes the addict can stop and implies condemnation if she does not.

May concludes his definition by referring to a person's will and desire. Desires may come from various parts of the psyche that are oriented to please others or to do the right thing or that draw on commonly held values. But the heart is the wheelhouse of the soul, the core of a human being where decisions are made. In the case of the addict, no matter the various attempts a person uses to draw from his feelings or his values or the things he has learned to try to turn away from the addictive impulse, the heart is held captive.

There is another captain onboard giving directions, and no attempts at trying to say no will be effective. The book *Alcoholics Anonymous*—produced by that organization and referred to as "the Big Book"—says that the alcoholic "will be absolutely unable to stop drinking on the basis of self-knowledge,"[4] and that is the truth for all addicts. Self-awareness alone is not enough, because someone (something) else is in charge of the person's heart.

Addiction Is Not an Excuse

In no way does being an addict excuse a person from her behavior. Understanding how addiction works is not to dismiss a person's responsibility for her life. On the other hand, understanding how addiction works is essential for realizing just what a challenge an addict is up against. It explains why a person's bad behavior does not respond to normal attempts at self-control. Understanding addiction explains why an addict does not—and indeed, cannot—respond the way most people do when they try to conform to commonly agreed-upon standards of appropriate behavior.

If I were not an addict, I may read the previous few paragraphs and say to myself, "Addicts are just making excuses for themselves." But it is just the opposite. While self-understanding alone will not heal us, rarely can we make the challenging journey to health and sobriety without adequate self-understanding. Most of us have to know what it is we're up against and why. Compulsive people who are moving toward health stop scapegoating their shame and stop making excuses. We try to acknowledge where the source of our hurt lies within us, because the remarkable reality of almost every single addict is that, try as we might to shortcut feelings and block out pain, we are never far away from our guilt and shame.

Occasionally I've run across people who are expressing significant difficulty in their lives and/or are causing it for others by their high-level narcissism. Now, every addict has some narcissistic qualities. When I was in the throes of my acting-out life, I certainly was narcissistic. It was evidenced this way:

every time I gave over to my compulsion, I was ignoring the needs and feelings of my wife, my children, my friends and my church. I was being selfish. As the Big Book of AA says, "Addiction is a case of self-will run riot."[5] But there is all the difference in the world between being narcissistic and being a narcissist. They are entirely different categories of disorder. All humans are capable of being more or less selfish (*narcissistic*), but we fluctuate up and down the spectrum. When I was acting out the most, I was fairly high on the spectrum of selfishness; but much of the rest of the time I was quite genuinely centered on the needs of others. On the other hand, a *narcissist*—the person who suffers from Narcissistic Personality Disorder—is motivated by a deep-seated and consuming need to be perceived by others as important. Even though they may be intelligent, high-achieving and even charming, they subtly use and manipulate others to achieve status and recognition. They do not move up and down the selfish spectrum as others do. The true narcissist has thrown some switch in the soul that totally blocks the pain he should feel from shame. The addict, on the other hand, doesn't have any switch. They addict is never truly apart from his sense of guilt and shame.

Never in my life was acting out okay to me. Never did I give in to the thought that, well, this is just the price of my giftedness, or, well, I do so much to serve others and I have to have some sort of break. Being broken in my sexual practices was never okay with me. That's why shame and self-loathing were my constant companions for more than forty years.

I don't think it is an easy thing for people who do not struggle with compulsive behavior to understand people who do. Of course it seems too strange. Why can't addicts just decide that they want to be different? Every addict I have ever met, ever worked with, ever seen recover or ever known until they disappeared into the abyss of self-destruction—every single one of them wished they could be different. Why is it they couldn't recover, or why is it that their journey to wholeness required a different path? These are important questions for all addicts to ask themselves.

So I was a person with anger, depression, anxiety, impulsiveness and compulsive sexual behaviors, and all that was incorporated into what I felt was a monstrous shadow of my personality. There was one more aspect of my life that, though it would eventually provide the help I needed to resolve the incongruities in my life, made my journey more challenging in some ways.

First Steps Out

I was married and a father. I was also a Christian. I served on Young Life staff. I earned two degrees from seminary and twice served as the moderator of our regional church body. I was a pastor who really believed what he preached. For multiple reasons I felt enormous guilt. Never in my journey did I dismiss the behaviors coming out of my dark nature as something to be ignored or tolerated. Never did I think it was okay for me to have this hidden life. Never did I play the game of rationalizing that because I was such a good teacher, such an inspirational speaker, such a caring and helpful person, this dark thing in me just had to be accepted and was the price of being gifted. *It was never okay.*

Shame and self-loathing were my constant companions all my life. And never were my shame and self-loathing more intense than when I preached, when I ministered to others and when I performed the functions of an ordained clergyman.

In 1990, the church Pam and I had planted was only a year old. We had four small children. I was exhausted. A good friend invited me on a four-day, silent, guided retreat. It was five of us with author and speaker Brennan Manning. This retreat and its setting proved to be God's brilliant intervention in my life that enabled me to take my first steps out of isolation toward eventual healing.

Knowing Brennan as I came to know him over the next few years, there couldn't have been a safer person to share my entire story with; but I didn't know him that well yet, and I was far too scared to tell him everything. In the time alone with him for spiritual direction, I was open enough that he figured out how much I was hurting.

We were retreating in a house on the grounds of a Benedictine convent in rural northern Missouri. Two miles away was Conception Abbey, a community of Benedictine monks. Brennan suggested a pathway for me to begin to break down my wall of isolation: he said I should have a priest hear my confession.

I walked over to Conception Abbey on a cold, sunlit December day. The priest who met me—I don't remember his name—took me into a room and listened as I stumbled through the list I had painstakingly made the night before of all the things I had done and for which I was so sorry. He was kind and gentle. He told me he couldn't offer me the Sacrament of Reconciliation as I was not Catholic, but he did say some words and then he prayed for me. He gave me a blessing. He was Christ to me in that moment, and I began to experience the grace of God in a new and profound way.

He gave me a warm hug, and when I left his presence, I walked out of the main building at Conception and across the driveway to a small grotto where there was a statue of Jesus and the Sacred Heart with an inscription below it: "Behold this heart which has loved men so much." Indeed. I sank into the grass and wept for a long, long time.

This encounter of grace would not solve all my problems or unravel all my garbled wiring. But God conveyed to me, through Brennan, through the retreat and through the Benedictine priest, the grace and encouragement I would need again and again and again for my journey through sexual addiction to genuine transformation.

Two years later, in the early part of 1992, I was still exhausted, scared, guilty and ashamed. While helpful, the experiences of the retreat were not enough. I was rigorously maintaining my hidden struggle with compulsive sexual behaviors. I told my wife that I thought I should probably go to a counselor for my anger. She readily agreed, which tells you how bad my struggle with anger was. Because we were a young couple in ministry raising four children, there wasn't money in our monthly budget for counseling fees. But I gulped hard and kept an appointment I'd made with a reputable Christian counselor in our city.

I was fully honest with him about my struggles, including my sexual issues. I was terribly anxious about what his reaction would be. So much of my life was about controlling the opinion others had of me, and now I was intentionally giving away that control. I was sure that who I was and how I behaved was so bad that any normal person would find me offensive and disgusting.

Just as God provided emotional relief through the Benedictine priest, he did so again through this therapist, who showed no discomfort with or disapproval of what I shared about myself. He was sensitive and he was accepting. He asked a lot of questions, and I did a lot of honest answering. At the end of the first session, he said that it was clear to him I was struggling with depression and that there was probably a lot about my childhood we needed to discuss.

The Problem of Being a Christian

While I suppose people who become ordained church leaders have various motivations for pursuing ministry, for me, becoming a pastor was a response to a profound sense of personal conviction and divine call. In high school and most of college, I thought I'd be a high-school English teacher. When a couple of close friends told me they thought I had abilities that should be used in ministry, it caused me to consider my emerging passions for God, for the things of God and for helping others connect and deepen their connection with God.

In my family, we attended church every week, but we never talked about God or Jesus or personal aspects of the faith. Occasionally my mother would talk about the choir's singing or some other part of the service and church life, but faith was never discussed. Yet I developed a keen God-consciousness. Several times at youth church camp or during a specific service, I had a distinct awareness of God. That awareness became very important to me. I thought being respectful of God and figuring out more about him and pleasing him were probably very important things to do. I really believed in God. God was important to me. But God had not yet become personal to me.

And then he did. He became intensely personal during my high-school years. I went with a couple of friends to visit another church's youth ministry, and at a summer evening Bible study in 1972 I had a profound spiritual awakening. Without knowing the language or issues involved, my faith found its footing and voice in the evangelical subculture.

By using the term *evangelical,* I mean an approach to Christian faith that highly values God and the Bible, as well as an understanding that Jesus Christ was both a real, historic human and the full expression of God at the same time in the same person, and that his life was a mission of rescuing lost loved ones. Then those of us who come to understand and believe these things live accordingly, including sharing these truths with others, genuinely loving them in practical ways. This expression of Christianity is also thoroughly trinitarian, believing in the mind-stretching concept that God makes himself known to us as three distinct and inextricably linked personal expressions: the Father, the Son and the Holy Spirit.

I write all this because being a Christian actually made some aspects of my struggle harder. I came to understand that in following Jesus, what we do with our life matters. What we do with our body matters. Early on I came to the conclusion that my compulsive sexual behavior was neither appropriate nor acceptable. I lusted most of the time, and my sexual distractions and desires were constant. I knew this wasn't right, but I couldn't stop. I mean *I could not stop.* No matter how I tried, no matter what I tried and no matter how much I prayed, I returned to my compulsive behaviors. I was becoming an addict—a term we overuse now and thereby cheapen and rob of its usefulness. What I mean by becoming an addict is that the overwhelming sense of euphoria I experienced during the short-term gratification created relief and distraction from my overarching sense of emptiness. Recognizing this intoxicating combination of relief and exhilaration, my brain demanded more so as to stabilize a sense of well-being. To maintain some sense of stability in my system, I became dependent on a habit that made me feel guilty and ashamed. I became an addict. So, my addiction and my faith went to war, and my soul was the battlefield.

How was it a battlefield? Because I knew the way I was living privately was incongruous with what I genuinely believed, my situation was intolerable to me. Yet I could not find a way to change my behaviors. And the context in which I was living gave me the message that there are issues that we do not discuss, that we handle them on our own. I felt very guilty, and I think it was appropriate, healthy guilt. My faith offered me genuine forgiveness, but I continued to engage in behaviors I could not understand or stop. And my faith context had no help to offer me. I felt very, very alone in my struggle; that loneliness fed my growing compulsive desires; and the constant sense of guilt fed my sense of being a shame-filled, shame-deserving person.

One of the most important things I've learned is that I was not and I am not alone. There are thousands of other clergy with this struggle, and hundreds of thousands of well-intentioned Christians struggle with guilt, shame and fear—all hiding their secret lives. Can this be what Christ wants for his church? Absolutely not.

I believe ministry leaders who are struggling with compulsive behaviors can find healing and freedom. I believe that in most cases they do not have to leave ministry to do so. I believe they cannot possibly do this alone, hiding in isolation. They need help. They need community. And they need the church they serve to help them. And I believe it's in the church's best interests to change the way she approaches sexually compulsive behavior and to help everyone who's struggling with it.

2

Sexuality and Spirituality

In the beginning, God created the heavens and the earth.
The earth was without form and void, and darkness was over
the face of the deep. And the Spirit of God was hovering
over the face of the waters.

When God created man, he made him in the likeness of God.
Male and female he created them, and he blessed them
and named them Man when they were created.

—GENESIS 1:1-2; 5:1-2

It might seem highly incongruous to some people that a person can be a growing, earnest Christian—especially a spiritual leader like a minister, priest or pastor—and also struggle with compulsive sexual behaviors. For years I was sure I was the only person in my church, in my clergy associations and among my Christian friends who did. It was startling to discover later that far more pastors struggle with compulsive sexual behaviors than don't.[1] How can that be? I think one of the factors is that there is a profound link between our spirituality and our sexuality.

Human sexuality is a fascinating aspect of being human.

Every human is a sexual being. "Our sexuality is the most private, the most intimate, the most idiosyncratic manifestation of who we are," writes Mark Patrick Hederman. "It is as personal and as unique as our fingerprint. It tells us the secret of our deepest identity."[2] Our sexuality and our expression of our sexuality can cause us to experience good feelings, great frustration, sublime satisfaction, fear, excitement and deep hurt.

Our culture, however, is absolutely schizophrenic and hypocritical about sex. We use sex to sell products and entertain each other. Sex is everywhere in our ads and movies and TV shows and talk-show conversations. When terrible sex crimes happen, there is an outcry against the evil of the behavior and the tragedy suffered by the victims. But if you look closely, there's also a keen, almost prurient, interest in the details. Even as we're horrified, we want to know what happened. Think about how many network and cable shows carry detailed information about sex-tainted crimes, acts and behaviors. There is a huge market for it. We're fascinated by sexuality—ours and others'.

The hypocrisy of our culture around sexuality borders on the bizarre. If someone crosses one of a very few taboo lines related to sexual behavior, he becomes a pariah to be locked away and shunned. I'm thinking of a local case in which a young man of eighteen and his girlfriend one year younger had sex. The girl's mother found out and contacted authorities, and the young man was charged with a sex crime, did two years in the state penitentiary and is now a registered sex offender. Is this right? Or have we lost perspective and are we overreacting as a culture?

My point is, it's human to have challenges and difficulties in understanding and handling our sexuality. We have to continually think clearly and carefully about what it means to be a sexual person and how to appropriately treat our sexuality in relation to others.

I stumbled into the world of sexual imagining and self-gratification in early adolescence, at least ten years before I met my wife and twenty-five years before I finally began the journey out of that wilderness. Pursuing and marrying Pam was perhaps the first significant thing I did to move from unhealthy living to healthy living. I'll never fully know what it cost her to marry me, but I know marrying her was the best thing that ever happened to me.

As we got to know each other and decided to marry, we had many things in common, especially our faith. But we had stark differences too. Pam comes from a relatively healthy family, and she had a very healthy approach to human sexuality. My family was dysfunctional and kept secrets. Hers was more open.

I had the erroneous notion that once Pam and I were married and intimate with each other, my sexual thinking and behaving would fall in line. But I'd already cultivated my default pattern of handling life, and I couldn't break it. This meant that for the first fifteen years of our marriage—because I kept my struggles hidden from her—Pam had an unseen presence in her marriage to me. It caused us a great deal of hurt and pain and struggle.

We had no way of understanding what was going on in our marriage. No one talked about sexually compulsive behavior; there were no books about it at the time, and our faith community never talked about sex except in a romanticized, idealized way. We needed help understanding what was going on, and the help wasn't there. We needed a lot of things to find our way out of my wilderness, and a realistic, genuinely Christ-based view of sexuality would have helped us a great deal.

The Gospel and Thinking About Sexuality

The gospel of Jesus is the story about God, about how much he loves his creation and about the extraordinary lengths to which he's gone to reconnect human beings to himself. The dimensions of our Creator's extravagant love are given fullness of expression in the story of Jesus of Nazareth, the God-Man who is the central figure in human history and whose self-giving life has opened the path for all men and women to live in increasing awareness of and intimacy with God. Through the living and dying and living again of Jesus, women and men are given the opportunity to so connect with the Spirit of their Creator that they actually become his agents of creativity and restoration. Living in this spiritual relationship and continuing the ministry of Jesus is what is meant by living in the kingdom of God.

Those who work at living in active, thoughtful partnership with the Spirit of God are the ones who constitute the real church. Lots of folks who are baptized and attend or are listed on the membership rolls of churches have no serious thought about following Christ. They're loved by God all the same, but they're not really Christians in the sense that they are not intentionally trying to conform their lives to Christ. Being a Christian is an affair of the heart—an interior sense of identity and being that spills into all aspects of life.

It is essential to note that the gospel is inherently corporate rather than individualistic. It is about who we are to be as a people here, not where we will end up as individuals. Too many American Christians live as if the primary point of the gospel is that we be "saved" for the next life. Having been assured of life in heaven after this life, they live now as if they are free to control their own devices and development.

Having the God of Jesus' gospel come into our life means a change, a different kind of life, the kind of experience here and now that could never happen without God. It's not about perfection. It's not about pretending. It's not about mustering a new morality that fits with a new worldview and a new set of values.

Living with the gospel in our heart means taking the life of Jesus into our very heartbeat and letting the life force of his Spirit season and salt, alter and redirect the ways we think and what we do with our feelings. All of that eventually begins to change how we live.

Living the gospel is a partnership between the redeeming Creator and repentant creatures. It is a joint effort that results in transformation. It is the transcendent becoming immanent, sort of in a lowercase way, just as Jesus coming into the world was the transcendent becoming immanent. And when that happens, the world notices. Why? Because people are hungry for a life genuinely touched from beyond. They are hungry for hope bigger than themselves.

Jesus does make it clear that eventually a winnowing will take place, that unfortunately not everyone is going to respond to his wildly generous offer of life transformation through grace and truth. But he's equally clear that the separating out of who's who and what's what is not *our* job. And as his message creates division, it really is only exposing divisions that are already there. What his message actually does is create a new people, a new family, a new community.

It also seems clear to me that the gospel is not about our living comfortable lives in this world. That might be one reason so much about the gospel doesn't make us feel very good. The truth is that the gospel is incredibly good for us. It's just that we often confuse what is comfortable and easy and pleasing with what is necessary and good and ultimately satisfying. The gospel doesn't satisfy my selfish whims of wanting life to be easier than it is. But the gospel makes me part of something so world-shatteringly awesome that sometimes I simply can't sit still thinking about it.

What does the gospel have to say, though, about my struggle

with sexual brokenness? What does it say about the struggle others have with their sexual brokenness? The verses at the head of this chapter remind us that our humanity is a reflection of our Creator, and our sexuality is an aspect of our humanity. Our sexuality is God-given and God-reflecting. Human sexuality is a beautiful, powerful gift from our Creator.

It may be that, because our sexuality is so wonderful, so important, so central to what it means to be human, that is the very reason we have such great trouble with it. We don't rightly understand what it means to be human and spiritual and sexual. We take our sexuality for granted. We misunderstand our sexuality in that we think of it only erotically. But to be masculine or feminine is much more than to express oneself erotically. Our sexuality provides us a way of feeling about life and seeing and interacting with others, but eros is only one aspect of it.

In our culture today, we know how to use sex for lots of things, but we don't understand how it works or what to do when someone has trouble with her sexuality. And one way or another, almost all people have some trouble with their sexuality.

If we take the gospel of Jesus and apply it to how we think about the sexual offenses of other people, when we're really honest about it, we hear the Holy Spirit gently whisper in our souls, "You're broken too." In the eyes of heaven, we are all offenders of sorts. That is why Jesus was clear that if we want to live his way and follow in his steps with his Father as our Father, it's important that we not judge others (see Matthew 7:1-5). And if the demands of the gospel seem like more than we can handle, Jesus reminds us that his Father desires mercy, not sacrifice (see Matthew 9:13). Mercy is a keynote of Jesus' ministry in the world, in our lives and in our relationships.

One of the most disappointing things about our current

struggles with cultural sexual brokenness is that in the very arena of divine and human interaction, the very place where we ought to find the most help with our sexual self-expression, too often we find the least. The church is meant to be a community of spiritual nurture and healing. But most of the time it avoids or misapplies how the gospel addresses being human and being sexual. The result is devastating. The church needs to recover her heritage of truth and grace and apply it to sexuality.

Sexuality, Spirituality and Human Fulfillment

Our spirituality and our sexuality are intimately linked; in fact, our sexuality issues from our existence as spiritual beings. Rather than being dualistic creatures with a spiritual nature and a physical nature, we're designed to be fully integrated beings. I did not understand this at all when I was younger. And by the time I began to grasp some of this thinking, compulsivity had already taken hold in my thinking and behaving, and I needed help rooting it out and dealing with it. Coming to understand the link between sex and spirit has been very important as I recover a true sense of what it means to be a healthy spiritual, sexual person.

When I speak of us as spiritual beings, I mean that we have an interior nature that permeates our physical and our emotional/mental being and is capable of integrating the various elements of what it means to be a person *and* is able to transcend the limits of our physical nature, principally by connecting with our Creator. Our spirit is not substantive, but it is meant to express itself in all we have that is substantive. God creates us as spiritual beings, and our sense of being spiritual is what I think of as our *heart*. Our heart is where the deepest, truest sense of our self is.

It is out of our heart (or spirit) that we make our best decisions. But we don't always or even usually do that. Often we unnecessarily have divisions between our truest values and our patterns of thinking, reacting and behaving. For most of us, our default decision making is not from a well-cultivated spiritual healthiness but from patterns of thinking and feeling that are largely reactive to what's going on around and within us.

God gives us a spirit encased in a soul and body, out of which we may fulfill our most noble purposes. God our Creator is intensely personal and intensely complex. God is a marvelously complex being far, far beyond our ability to comprehend. But he has made us in his image, and he has given us the capacity to have a meaningful, moment-by-moment connection with him.

Many of us call God "Father," and we may use the masculine pronoun for God because in the Judeo-Christian faith, God has revealed himself in a patriarchal culture. And it's useful to have one gender to use in the English language. But I think it's clear that God in his nature is far beyond our thinking of masculine and feminine. Both our masculinity and our femininity find their source in God and are expressions of God in us. God is feminine and masculine and more—so very much more. We relate to God out of our masculinity and femininity, and the relational familiarity we share helps us grow in our relationship with God. Knowing God and having a relationship with him is why we live and where we find our real life.

God makes us to know him and makes us like him. And in this he makes us spiritual beings (like him) and physical beings (like him). He makes us spiritual in that there is a substance to us that is far beyond what we see and touch and know in the concrete. Why do we understand and appreciate the reality of transcendence, even yearn for it, except that we reflect it and were made for it? We are creatures that understand and have a facility for that which is over us and beyond us and within us all at the same time.

Walk down a Midwestern street in late October, when the air is crisp and cool, when the sky is laden with quiet clouds and the trees are shouting colors with stunning vibrancy. Alive with the physical, in those moments we can feel the breeze on our faces and smell the change of seasons and know—know!—that we are touching and being touched by a rhythm of life far beyond ourselves.

Sit on the beach or shore and look at the immensity of the ocean. Feel the mist, hear the pounding of the surf, smell the salt, and ponder the enormity of what lies before you. You see it and apprehend it physically, yet if you're paying attention, you also sense it spiritually. There is something overwhelmingly huge at work, rhythmically pulling and pushing, soothing yet intimidating, hinting at a power that could bless or curse. We are made for transcendence.

We are also physical creatures, made to sense and feel and touch, to express our spirituality in tangible ways. One of those ways is to understand, inhabit and express our sexuality. As humans, we are sexual creatures. It's part of what makes us spiritual creatures. God at his very core makes himself known to us as a community, as a society of interpersonal self-expression within himself—the Trinity.

So as God's creatures, made in some way to reflect him, we are created to commune, to connect with each other. Our sexuality is an essential aspect of how we do our self-expressing and connecting. Rob Bell understands that sexuality is a wonderful, all-encompassing aspect of ourselves. He writes, "For many, sexuality is simply what happens between two people involving physical pleasure. But that's only a small percentage of what sexuality is. Our sexuality is all of the ways we strive to reconnect with our world, with each other, and with God."[3]

In *Simply Christian,* British author and pastor N. T. Wright examines four areas of current human existence and experience that point us to the ancient and present love and design of our Creator. These four areas are echoes of the Creator's voice resonating in his lost but loved creatures: the longing for justice; the quest for spirituality; the hunger for relationships; and the delight in beauty.[4] When discussing the third, the hunger for relationships, he has this to say about sex:

> At the heart of relationships we find sex. Not, of course, that all relationships are sexual in the sense of involving erotic behavior. . . . And yet when human beings relate to one another, they relate as male and female; maleness and femaleness are not identities which we only assume when we enter into one particular kind of relationship (namely, a romantic or erotic one). Here, too, we all know in our bones that we are a particular kind of creature, and yet that we find it difficult to handle *being* this kind of creature.[5]

Sexual Brokenness

Given the sphere in which we live and the sort of people we are, it's difficult for us to get this all straightened out. Something within us all is desperately broken, and often our spirituality and our sexuality become disjointed; we may find it difficult to integrate the two. While I think God created us to be holistic creatures, meaning that what we do with our thoughts, feelings and bodies reflects the values and grounding of our spirits, most of us are fractured in how we live. We have difficulty sometimes even thinking about sexuality as a good and wonderful aspect of our selves.

Maybe we lack the vision for an integrated life, or maybe we've never been given the tools. Maybe we've been abused or damaged and we can't find the congruency we were designed for. Maybe we're too much in a hurry to accomplish something or become someone. Maybe we're oriented just to get what we want when we feel the impulse. Whatever it is, we're all broken and we all struggle. And whatever the reasons, our abuse of our sexuality is creating great hurt and destruction for lots of people inside and outside the church.

What difference does it really make, we must ask ourselves, if a lot of adults are finding sexual gratification in all sorts of ways? Just because it isn't happening in the bedrooms of people married to each other, is there really a problem here? Why is anyone else's behavior our problem?

People can be in deep distress without consciously registering distressful feelings. Sexual brokenness hurts people—the people who are sexually broken and most of the people around them as well. One of the big lies about human sexuality—human life, really—is that there aren't consequences. Most of us agree that if someone shoots a gun at someone and injures or kills her, that's not a good use of personal freedom. There ought to be consequences for that sort of thing. But sex? Other than pedophilia and rape, what difference does sexual behavior make, really?

It turns out that it makes a huge difference what we do with our sexuality, because it comes out of who we are and what we're doing with what we've been given. And we're all connected to each other, so what we do with our lives impacts others.

Look again at the big picture we're each a part of. God gives us life. He makes us spiritual beings and sexual beings, and a lot of our living is a bit disordered. We live in a world that doesn't work right a good deal of the time, and it doesn't work right largely because of how people live. Okay, tornadoes and earthquakes and natural disasters are another category of living in a disordered realm, but most of the real suffering happens because people can be so difficult, destructive and indifferent.

Sexual Brokenness, Lust and Pornography

God creates us as sexual and spiritual beings, and when we are fully integrated, we function well. But few of us are fully integrated beings, so we often misunderstand and misuse our God-given desire to connect with others. We have the right impulse not to be alone, to connect, but we struggle with this because our natures are flawed. We don't always live the way we were designed or even desire to live. Because we are spiritually broken people, we engage in disordered living.

If we're disordered in our hearts, our approach to connecting is fractured. This brings us to lust. We lust when we co-opt something or someone to meet a legitimate desire we have in a way that honors neither us nor the person/thing we desire. Lusting is fragmented living. Lusting comes out of desires that are normal—even God-given—but our bent vision and short-cutting strategies mean that even when we attain what we desire, we do not find fulfillment or contentment.

For us to live lives of wholeness and goodness, lust must be surrendered to love. And that means a death of sorts. If lust has become our way of expressing our desire to connect with others, we must die to it so that we may take up a healthier way of living. C. S. Lewis wrote, "Lust is a poor, weak, whimpering, whispering thing compared with that richness and energy of desire which will arise when lust has been killed."[6]

Pornography is a tool for facilitating lust. I discovered the realities of sexual attraction and sexual imagining, and then learned I could cultivate those thoughts into an imaginary world of my making. It was powerful and intoxicating. And when I discovered images that excited my erotic imagination, it was like pouring gas on a fire.

Pornography takes something very real, very human—something everyone can relate to—and distorts it. Our sexuality is meant to be lived and expressed in the context of a healthy, integrated life, and pornography is never an expression of good health or integrated living. Pornography is dis-integrating. While our sexuality is but one aspect of who we are as human beings and needs to be integrated with our other aspects, pornography isolates that one human dimension and distorts it by magnifying it and minimizing it at the same time.

That pornography distorts our humanity is what no one in the sex industry seems to admit, and most of us who have used the products of the sex industry for our own gratification don't see it or don't want to admit it either. Saying that porn cheapens our sexuality doesn't go far enough. Porn magnifies human sexuality, distorts it, makes it larger than reality and isolates it for trade—I'll show you this and you give me that. At the same time, it makes the magnificence of being a creature made in the image of God something as insignificant as ink on paper or pixels on a screen. It's a most malicious smearing of the divine image in us. Simply put, porn is uncompromising, progressive, destructive evil.

What about the seemingly harmless nature of innocuous sexual gratification? Whom does it hurt? It hurts the women and men who work in the sex trade. It hurts those who patronize the sex trade. It hurts those who live with or care about them.

We are dynamic beings. We grow and change, acquire and adapt. The things that root in our psyches grow and change too. Some people can dabble a bit in pornography or experiment with sexual adventures and then turn away, seemingly unaffected, and leave them behind. Even in these cases, though, we are touched and affected by what we do with who we are, and there is an impact. Nothing we repeatedly expose ourselves to is without effect. William Struthers writes, "Repeated exposure to any stimulus results in neurological circuit making. That is how we learn."[7]

Pornography has a progressive effect, that is, what excites a person at first won't create the same arousal later. We start in one place, or with one passing notion, and find ourselves moving into areas where we never dreamed we'd find ourselves. Increasing numbers of us are moving from infrequent use of porn or other methods of sexual gratification to frequent use to compulsive use. This is because compulsive sexual behavior is an arousal addiction, and so a person not only needs more, they need different stimulus to maintain arousal.

Sexual Addiction Is a Spiritual Disease

How is it that something as good and beautiful and wonderful as our sexuality can be turned into something as punishing and depriving as sexual addiction? We have to look at the link between spirituality and sexuality. All of us have the nature—the shared human nature—to misuse the gifts of God. Part of our human journey is to learn to harness our appetites and our desires to appropriate uses of the gifts in our lives. We don't let our two-year-olds put their little fingers in electrical outlets, and we don't let our ten-year-olds have pizza every night of the week. We train them to live within appropriate boundaries. But all of us have a nature that wants to jump the curb from time to time.

Because we are spiritual people, because we are made in God's image, we are vulnerable to sexual addiction. God makes us spiritual beings, and he gives us the ability to create things and do work. We apply our efforts and energies to alter circumstances. Just as we can use these powers for good, we can also use them as illegitimate solutions to our situations. Some of us inadvertently, unknowingly, create a subpersona within our souls. We take our vulnerable personality and the right (wrong) combination of shortcutting behaviors, and within the fascinating matrix of the human soul we create an addictive personality. I made a little Tommy, and he's mine to let run (and ruin) things or he's mine to control. I didn't choose to become an addict. But I made choices that resulted in my addictive nature birthing an addictive persona. None of us chooses our addiction, but we can make choices to recover.

Being an addict, any kind of addict, is taking an aspect of our lives and misusing our God-granted powers of creation to develop a coping system that displaces the care our Creator desires to give us himself. All of us do this. But addicts take it to the extreme. That's why addicts are just like everyone else, only more so.

The point is that our struggle with compulsive sexual behaviors comes to us honestly. Sexuality is a wonderful and powerful gift. It is one of the flaws of being human to misuse our gifts. I have the ability to speak well, but sometimes I speak in a way that helps people and other times I speak in a way that hurts. All things belong to God. God makes us co-creators with himself. In the wrong circumstances, we create addictive subpersonas, and once they're born, we have to deal with them the rest of our lives.

In the next dimension, Christ will finally and fully make all things new; but while we remain in this dimension, our spiritual/sexual self-creations remain with us. It is the powerful promise of the gospel of Jesus that, as dire as this seems, we are not yet doomed. In fact, we may just find ourselves in the place where Jesus and his gospel can have a most magnificent and redemptive impact. That is good news, indeed.

Living in an Addiction-Prone World

At the end of it, addiction is about shortcuts that become life-consuming ruts. People in our culture are more and more over-loaded with demands, with sensory stimulation, with options and with boredom. Less and less are we as a people prepared to or expected to reflect, to quiet ourselves, to live within rea-sonable boundaries and means. We live in a culture of excess. We are pitched excessive expectations, such as when sports broadcasters over-hype athletic contests as the "game of the century." (By strict definition can't that only happen once every hundred years and wouldn't we need to wait until the hundred years are over before we can call a game that?) We have ex-cessive resources. Compared to the experiences of most humans in other cultures, both in history and today, we enjoy vast of-ferings of food, entertainment and living comforts. We have acquired excessive appetites. We are pummeled with multi-media advertisements exhorting us to buy products which will fill us with satisfaction, entertain us or make others want to be us. Ever spend time absent-mindedly staring in your refrig-erator looking for something to capture your imagination? And we live in a culture of excessive demand. We need to look better, be attractive, lose weight or achieve more. It is a culture of excess based on dissatisfaction and elusive contentment. To find relief, we cut corners. Compulsive behaviors offer shortcuts, ways to numb out or dumb out and not feel.

Others of us are overloaded with guilt and shame. It may be true guilt; we have behaved in a way that has created genuine difficulty or suffering for another. More often, in a culture in-undated with family systems that are grossly dysfunctional, it's false guilt (shame) we struggle with. Shame has tremendous power—truly crippling power—in a person's soul and life. It is so overwhelming that, just like excess, it creates a dynamic in which we are prone to look for an escape. So, look for more and more people to develop shortcuts. More and more people will suffer from compulsive behaviors.

When Jesus began his public ministry, he made clear to those who would believe in him and follow him that part of his agenda was to set free those held captive by the things that lock us away from the grace of God. I was captive to a compulsive use of sexual thinking and behaving. And I longed for freedom, longed for transformation. As my life continued, I yearned to become a person who lived a healthy and appropriate life. No doubt my life worked in many ways, and in some ways it worked exceedingly well. But in other ways, it was confounding to me. I was angry. I was depressed. I was trapped. And I was alone.

People who suffer from compulsive behaviors are impaired in their ability to have healthy, intimate relationships. We don't know how to do intimacy. We don't know how to relate to others in free, open, healthy ways. We get sidetracked by our interior motives and impulses and are often blindsided by the ulterior motives of others. We know how to relate chaotically, but relating in calm ways eludes most of us. I think this is true of everyone who struggles with addictive behavior, but nowhere is it more crippling than with compulsive sexual behavior. Sexual addicts are truly impaired in their ability to experience true intimacy.

Though intimacy impairment is part of the affliction of sexual addicts, it would be wildly inaccurate to think of sexual addicts as lacking people skills. Quite the contrary. Most of us have learned to excel in several aspects of relating to others. We learn how to negotiate many of life's demands, and this means we often can deal with other people in healthy, appropriate ways. I learned how to counsel others, listen to folks after worship services, pray with people who are struggling and make helpful, if brief, hospital visits. I was very good at spiritual direction, really very good with people generally. So where was my intimacy impairment? It was in the wall I'd built, the lack of integration in my life. I was never able to be fully present and fully integrated for a lengthy period.

Early in my journey, I knew using pornography was not a good thing for me. I knew it wasn't a good thing for anyone. I had a sense of guilt because I'd learned it was not acceptable in my religious circle. But I had no idea how it worked, how it triggered a crippling dependency in me—and does the same in others. I needed to learn more about addiction and its self-reinforcing cycles.

3

Coming to Know the Enemy Within

The Spirit of the Lord is upon me,
because he has anointed me
to proclaim good news to the poor.
He has sent me to proclaim liberty to the captives
and recovering of sight to the blind,
to set at liberty those who are oppressed,
to proclaim the year of the Lord's favor.

—JESUS, READING ISAIAH IN THE SYNAGOGUE
IN NAZARETH (LUKE 4:18)

It is almost impossible for someone who's never had to live a secret life to imagine what it takes to hide and the costs involved. You have to work hard to find time to give to your secret activities, and then you have to find excuses to cover the time you've used. Almost invariably it means shading the truth and outright lying.

Those who are not addicted to sex understandably assume that the addict at least experiences enjoyment from the sexual activity, but this is not the case. There is excitement, but as the compulsive life progresses, there is hardly any good feeling for the addict—only a mind-numbing, compulsive urge to seek relief and escape. And the demand for enough stimuli to satisfy escalates. What once sufficed no longer does. Lust always demands more from the person who uses it and never delivers joy. I lived with lust dominating my thoughts for a long time, and it was terribly draining. By the time I finally gave up trying to deal with my problems alone and went to a therapist in 1992, I was exhausted.

Robert Louis Stevenson's *Dr. Jekyll and Mr. Hyde* was written to describe the problem of opium addiction in Victorian London. Many aspects of what Stevenson described in Hyde's behavior and Jekyll's predicament match well with my struggles with compulsive sexual behaviors.

What did that struggle look like on a daily basis? Almost every day began with an interior argument along the lines of "I'm not going to mess up today." Nearly every day this self-coaching in my head was met with feelings of fatigue, anxiety or despair. Without the words consciously forming in my mind, I had a pervasive sense that "I don't have what it takes."

I would mentally review the day—my work and appointments and obligations. Not always, but usually, this review resulted in despair and hopelessness. Almost never could I recognize why I was feeling overloaded, despairing or hopeless. It was part of the natural terrain of my internal existence.

I looked for motivation to avoid thinking about sex. Sometimes I found it in work or activities that captivated my imagination and gave me purposeful energy. Most of the time that was not the case, however, so I fought the idea of using sexual thinking with my convictions of what I should be doing and how I should be thinking and how I ought to behave. Sometimes this worked, and I got through my day behaving in an appropriate way. More often it didn't.

Later, as I worked through therapy, I began to recognize several predictable triggers that made me much more vulnerable to obsessive searching for escape through sex. High stress was one trigger that caused me keen vulnerability. Another was boredom. A third trigger was opportunity: did my meetings and obligations take me to certain parts of town where it would be easy to look for porn and more tempting to engage in sexualized thinking? In those instances I had a diabolical conversation with myself, one voice urging me toward honest, truthful and obedient behaving and the other quietly mapping out possibilities for finding a break and exploring relief.

Whenever I used sexual thinking and behaving, a period of deep, deep despair, self-recrimination and disgust invariably followed, and then a sincere prayer of begging God for forgiveness and help. It was like finding myself in a pit of mud and slime, slowly trying to pull my soul out of the mess. I had to then try to refocus my energy and think about what I needed to do for my job and my family.

If there were similarities in my life to the struggle Stevenson wrote about, there was one notable exception: my Jekyll always remembered what my Hyde had been up to the night before. So there's another element of the truly divided life: struggling with the recurring weight of legitimate guilt and searing shame.

Half my life went to secret behaviors, the other half to public living. And half of that was focused on coping with the messes of the hidden half. That didn't leave much for doing the rest of my life. That's why compulsive people and addicts are usually so tired; they end up needing their "drugs" to prop them up to perform. It's an amazingly self-replicating way to destroy a life slowly.

This sort of life requires a person to learn to compartmentalize his beliefs and behaviors. Otherwise, the hypocrisy of repeatedly engaging in self-disrespecting and self-destructive behaviors is intolerable. To understand people who struggle with compulsive sexual behavior, you have to know that we begin building walls very early in life and usually for very good reasons. Somewhere early on, we become aware of the threat of pain and damage others will do to us—we know this is true because they already have done us damage and caused us pain—and the only way to protect ourselves is to learn to put our vulnerability out of their reach. So we build walls.

I imagine folks wonder why someone like me didn't just leave the ministry and at least minimize feeling like such a hypocrite. That is a good question, and the answer is complex. There are many reasons someone struggling with hidden compulsive behaviors finds the thought of leaving ministry overwhelmingly threatening. Leave ministry and do what? Your skill set is quite particular, so you don't have the bandwidth to change careers without stepping backward financially. Further, most males and some females highly identify with their work; it is what they do, how they contribute to the world and earn their way. If they leave ministry, who are they and what do they do?

Beyond "who am I" is the question of how to make it in life. Support myself how? If you're in Protestant ministry, you're most likely in debt from graduate studies and not making a significant salary. If you have dependents—and most of us do—the pressure to maintain your position and income is all the greater. Most clergy are barely making it financially, and leaving their ministry position without a clear path of providing for themselves and their families would be a disastrous move.

And how do you explain your need to leave ministry without saying why? Ministry is a highly relational environment; people will want to know why you're leaving, where you're going and what you're going to do. Most people who struggle with addiction and compulsive behaviors also have significant self-image issues and relational sensitivities that make the stay-or-go challenge all the more confusing.

More significant than anything I've mentioned is a person's sense of call. The thinking goes like this: Ministry is what I am supposed to do. If I leave, I'm being disobedient. I'm keenly aware of being disobedient in my personal behaviors, but leaving ministry won't free me from compulsive behaviors. I will be doubly disobedient! God wants us to be whole, to be obedient, to be helpful to others, to serve with integrity. That's what I want to do. It's just that I need help being the person I want to be while I do it, and I don't know how to find that help.

Finally, someone struggling with compulsive behaviors by her very nature has trouble with trusting others, thinking clearly and finding healthy ways to deal with inner conflict. It's simply not reasonable to think this person is going to be able to make clear and healthy decisions of such magnitude on her own. Everything has taught her to trust no one with the dark aspects of her life.

I'm not saying that is right, but it is the way we think. Perhaps this reasoning seems like making excuses, whining or blaming others for our own failures. I understand why some folks think that. And in reality, everyone who is working on stemming compulsive behaviors must develop a ruthless self-inventory of whining and fixing blame, and they must disengage from victim thinking. It's my life, and my mistakes and disasters are mine—no one else's.

I am describing real issues and the dumbfounding conundrum compulsion-bound clergy face. These are not excuses; these are the facts and dynamics thousands of men and women in ministry are struggling with every day, and they're struggling alone.

Work with addicts, and over and over you'll hear stories of abuse and victimization. Now, not all people who struggle with sexual addiction were abused as children and not all childhood sexual-abuse victims become sex addicts. Further, even if an addicted person is a survivor of childhood abuse, it is his responsibility to confront and deal with his own self-destructive and other-destructive behavior. We are not responsible for becoming addicts, but we are responsible for recovering. Recognizing origins of self-protective behavior does not excuse the damage we do as addicts. But it is helpful to recognize how predominant it is that someone struggling with a wall in her life built the wall for good reason. It was the only way to survive as a vulnerable child.

Survival of real and serious threats is a good reason to protect yourself. So if the wall is important in self-preservation, how threatening is it to think about tearing it down? Once it's gone, it's gone. Once it's out, it's out. Once you let others know you have a significant and particular weakness, you'll never be able to protect yourself that way again. When the relational hiding has been because of pain and exploitation, there will be strong internal and subconscious energy against openness. It's no easy thing to tear down our walls, to become open with others about who we really are and what we're doing in the hidden folds of our life.

Monkeys, Messes and Monsters

The path to human wholeness an addict must travel is different from that of people who aren't addicts, because the nature of his or her affliction has taken on different dynamics. All of us are flawed, all of us have selfish natures, all of us need to be forgiven and changed. All of us have a personal, human nature oriented in our natural humanity to be selfish, to think we know better than others, to be overly self-protective and to try to hide our deficiencies. What begins in infancy as somewhat innocuous sinful nature becomes a monkey on our backs as we grow.

Monkeys are very cute, I think. Think about times you've seen them on TV, dressed up in little outfits, riding tricycles, sitting at tables—acting like humans and carrying on. But it has occurred to me that I like to watch them when they're controlled, like in a good zoo setting or in the TV studio or set. It has to be quite different to actually live with one. I suspect it could be pretty chaotic. Imagine a monkey living with you and having the run of your place, playing with appliances and turning things over and traumatizing the kitty and pooping on the table. General mayhem.

I have a friend, Toby, who lived in the Sudan for a time and, through no intention of his own, came to have several monkeys share his home. When I asked him what it was like to have monkeys, he said it was a much worse situation than people might think. Pooping on the table is mild. Messes and chaos, yes, but the dirty little secret is that monkeys are skillful thieves with apparently no conscience. They have no sense of differentiation of what is yours and what is theirs. Toby told me that too many times he responded to a knock at his door to have one of his neighbors greet him with a determined face and a grim voice saying, "I am here to kill the monkey."

Our human nature is like having a pet monkey—seemingly not that bad, even cute sometimes. But it always poops on the table. It makes messes. And it embarrasses us.

Healthy Christian spirituality is about capturing our monkey and making it serve our interests. It is about harnessing the nature that is wildly selfish and bringing it under control under the direction of our Creator, so that we can live lives of love and service, happiness and joy. We all have monkeys; we all make messes. But for some of us, the particular monkeys we have are a different breed, and our vulnerabilities are of a different order, and the monkeys change on us. Because of personal wiring or our environment or both, what starts off as cute and sometimes annoying becomes threatening and tragic.

Flirting with our sexuality, playing around the edges of this powerful gift, is much like thinking we're playing with a cute little primate, an innocent, intelligent and playful partner that will give us mild and safe entertainment. That's what the use of sex in our culture seems to be for a lot of us—playful and cute most of the time. Oh, to be sure, sometimes our monkey puts its paws over our eyes while we're driving and it's hard to see. We might almost crash the car every now and again. And it does cost some money to feed and take care of the monkey. But we put up with it, even when it gets bigger and takes up more space on the sofa and time out of our day. Because it's so cute and it makes us laugh and makes us feel good, we tolerate it.

But for some of us—and as you read this, imagine you are hearing the dark, ominous tones of a horror movie soundtrack—what starts off as an idle curiosity takes up residence. What begins as a cute little monkey becomes a gorilla. It becomes bigger than we ever imagined, and instead of riding around on our backs, it throws us over its own back. Instead of going with us everywhere we go, it takes us places we never imagined going. Instead of pestering us for some of our time and attention, it forcefully demands our participation. We wake up— if we wake up—and find we are no longer free.

That is exactly what is happening in the life of person after person, family after family. Freedom is being lost to addiction— all sorts of addictions—and the worst, I think, is compulsive sexual behavior. That's because we are made the way we are; we are dynamic, growing, developing beings. But when our sexuality is broken and it isn't treated, it doesn't stay broken. It gets more broken.

A young boy discovers porn in his father's chest of drawers. At first he's stunned and excited. His heart races after a few stolen minutes, and he carefully puts it back. But he doesn't forget, and the next time he's bored or has the freedom, he sneaks a look again. When he reaches the age of sexual experimentation, he begins to masturbate to the images. This seems like an age-appropriate behavior. But introduce just one of many possible elements, and it becomes not only a useful but important and increasingly obsessive habit.

Maybe there's unhappiness in the home, and the escape with dad's porn offers relief. Or maybe the boy is too shy to develop healthy relationships, and so passing the time this way gives him a thrill instead of boredom. Maybe his mother is overbearing and he struggles with resentment; if the porn hits him in a certain way, it might scratch in places he didn't even realize he itched. All this to say, it becomes a habit. And for many young people, it becomes a habit they need. And then it becomes a habit they can't break, even if they try—especially when they try! The boy is now a man with an addiction. His brokenness grew, and he's no longer free.

A girl is at first befriended by a nice neighbor, but then it begins to be a little more. The neighbor is older, wiser, maybe a man who's really good with children or someone who works at her church. And there's an additional need: a missing parent, a family in crisis, a child not getting the sort of attention she was designed to get at this stage. So it comes from somewhere else, but it leads to other things. They become closer, dependent, intimate. The word is never used, the concept would be foreign to her, but she has been violated. Yet it's confusing because she has also felt something that seems to her to be very much like love. It's not love; it's abuse. And if it's not detected, not addressed and not replaced with real love, she'll live into her adult years repeating and recycling the abusive pattern. Her brokenness grows, and she's no longer free.

The Cycle of Addiction

All of us seeking recovery from compulsive sexual behaviors owe a huge debt of gratitude to Patrick Carnes. He has pioneered research and treatment for this addiction and has helped move forward our understanding and treatment of it. His *Out of the Shadows* (Hazelton, 2001) and *Don't Call It Love* (Bantam, 1991) are essential reading for anyone who would like to better understand compulsive sexual behavior.

Carnes helps us understand that the foundation of compulsive sexual behavior is a personal belief system that has some fundamental flaws. Whether because of environment or personal wiring or both, all addicts have a cluster of core beliefs, and these are the beginning of becoming an addict. They believe there is something wrong with them, that they are not okay people. They are convinced that others do not really care about them, or if they do, they wouldn't care if they really knew how bad the addict is. Addicts are convinced their struggle makes them unacceptable to others.

Eventually they add to their core beliefs that sexual expression offers them the only relief they will ever find and that life without it would simply be unbearable. This is the core of an addict's belief system, and it is what fundamentally differentiates a sex addict from a narcissist.

It would be unusual for an addicted person to know this is her core belief system without outside help. It is usually not until later that she might recognize these statements as the truths that guided her conscious and subconscious thought processes. Regardless, this is in fact the distorted belief system out of which comes impaired thinking.

At the top of the list of impairments is *denial*. So unbearable is the life of an addict and so keen is his sense of shame, denial is the only way to continue living. *It's just not that bad,* he thinks. *No one will ever know. It doesn't really matter what happens to me; if I die everyone else will be better off. Everyone does* something. *I'll never get sick from this. None of this matters.* And on and on and on.

Denial leads to rationalizations, arguments, self-justification and circular reasoning, all of which culminate in *self-delusion*. This is how a good person can find himself arguing with his spouse over a question she has about where he was or what he has been doing. He feels guilty and ashamed, but cannot let her know the truth, because the consequences are simply too threatening, and he'll fix it all anyway. So he lies and then expresses sincere love and devotion and intention for a better future without these misunderstandings. Before he knows it, the addictive personality within has fused his false life with his sincere desire to be a better person. All the while, the unaddicted spouse feels that she is in some crazy interaction and does not know what to believe. This is the madness of addiction.

But how does addiction cycle around in a person's life?[1] Faulty core beliefs lead to distorted thinking, which leads to the *addiction cycle,* which we'll look at in a moment. Once the addiction cycle has run one lap, the addicted person begins to lose the ability to manage her life. She has lost control. *Unmanageability* has begun, and life will never be the same. This self-perception of unmanageability is overwhelming. It is this sense that powerfully reinforces faulty core beliefs like *there is something wrong with me; I'm not okay; if people really knew who I was they'd never accept me; I am broken and worthless.* It is a self-reinforcing cycle of self-denigration.

Carnes offers a useful illustration of the life of an addicted person. Imagine two circles, one on top of the other, like two clock faces. They overlap where the top clock face is at six and the bottom clock face is at twelve. Now picture the above four elements: faulty core beliefs, impaired thinking, addiction cycle and unmanageability as four points on the top clock face: twelve o'clock, faulty core beliefs; three o'clock, impaired thinking; six o'clock, the addiction cycle; and nine o'clock, unmanageability. The way a compulsive person's mind works is that as the top clock hand moves from twelve to three to six, at six o'clock it swings to the lower circle or clock face. The addictive cycle (six o'clock on the top circle) has its own clock face with four positions. At twelve is preoccupation, at three is ritualization, at six is sexual compulsivity and at nine is despair.

Preoccupation is the place in the cycle where impaired thinking leads the person into a trance or mood in which his thinking becomes obsessed with escape. Life is simply intolerable. The pain and self-loathing and stress are too intense. The addict cannot manage it; he does not think he can survive without relief. Therefore he becomes preoccupied with looking for relief—and the addiction clock begins to run.

This leads to the second phase of the addiction cycle, *ritualization* (three o'clock), where the addict's mind begins to review and survey her routines for sexually acting out. This is self-grooming for the compulsive behaviors and intensifies the addict's desire/need for them. Actually, what we know now is that at this stage a dopamine drip has begun in the brain, and the addict is already feeling relief. But the relief—the dopamine drip—is absolutely dependent on the completion of the cycle. And just as important, the cycle is strengthened because of the dopamine drip, so the addict has no way out. Once any addict hits this stage, barring an external interruption of the cycle, it is nearly impossible for an addict not to progress on to the behavior.

The six o'clock phase is the *compulsive sexual behavior,* the goal of the cycle, the point of realizing relief. This provides a momentary release from all shame, all guilt, all stress and all pressure. For a few moments—and only a very few—the addict is free from a life of horror and self-loathing. And then in a crushing swing of the clock's hand, the addict finds herself at nine—*despair.* The good feeling evaporates suddenly, and the addict is left with the onrushing wave of *I am a despicable, horrible person.*

The addiction cycle now complete, the feelings of the compulsive person move seamlessly back from the bottom clock face to the top clock face, from the six to the nine o'clock position, *unmanageability.* And it starts all over. The compulsive person, awash in despair, shame and pain, is at twelve, faulty core beliefs: *I'm not okay. I'm unacceptable to others. If other people knew, they would totally reject me. How can I handle this miserable life?* And so on. The cycle reinforces itself, because the despair and unmanageability crush the addict and reinforce the faulty core beliefs of worthlessness, the need to hide and the demand for relief.

This might be the ultimate cruelty of addiction: the cycle reinforces itself and gives it strength. Think of the rings in the trunk of a huge oak tree. Every ring represents a complete set of seasons, and with each ring the tree grows taller and the roots grow deeper and the shade of the tree covers more ground. Each cycle of addictive thinking and acting deepens the addict's dependency on the "drug," spreads out the behavioral thinking and options, and covers more territory in the addict's life.

Neurochemistry and Crazy Living

In recent years, neurological research has filled in a lot of the blanks, explaining why the addiction cycle works the way it does. The brain secretes a wonderful drug, dopamine, which gives a sense of pleasure to us when we engage in certain activities.[2] That's a good thing. And if God through nature designed the dopamine release for helping a man and a woman strengthen their relationship with each other through the act of sexual intimacy, we've unfortunately learned to get that same buzz with shortcuts: sexual activities with people we aren't in a committed relationship with, pornography and other nonrelationship-based ways of getting sexually aroused.

We can co-opt the dopamine release by finding shortcuts to things that we use contrary to our own best interests. And, if we're engaging in risky behavior or compromising our principles and therefore incurring significant guilt and anxiety, we release adrenaline as well. The adrenaline can double or triple the impact of the dopamine. Can you see how a Christian or an addict engaging in self-threatening behaviors is unintentionally treating herself to a high-impact dose of neurochemicals that will serve to reinforce the behavior?

If that weren't enough, recent studies are showing that there is a natural pairing of dopamine release during sexual interaction between two people and the release of oxytocin after the sex act is concluded.[3] Oxytocin has a bit of a depressing impact, but not in a bad way. It causes a nurturing effect. As the oxytocin is released, a couple tends to relax from the dopamine high and connect with each other in a way that is complementary to the sex act they've just engaged in. It's a complete act of connecting, deepening their bond. It calms us so we cuddle.

So, what happens to someone swinging from one sex act to another, or one pornographic image to another? Dopamine hit after dopamine hit, but no natural bonding, no healthy descent. The oxytocin is still released, but no healthy bonding ensues. If we're using porn, we're left with a pronounced feeling of emptiness. If a person is using promiscuous sex with others instead of porn, the bonding process is interrupted when the relationship comes to an end. If a person is promiscuous or uses porn, he is increasingly less able to bond genuinely with a significant other and continues using sex to get high, but then feels emptier and emptier, which make him want the high all the more. It's a self-reinforcing cycle of personal self-destruction.

This gives us a biochemical explanation of why compulsive sexual behavior hooks some of us so firmly and at the same time traps us in the great lie. For no matter how much of a seemingly good thing we get, it will never result in satisfaction. Learning these things is helpful. It's important to know what we're up against. But knowledge alone is not enough to allow us to change. Change happens in the heart, and the heart is a complex thing.

But Why Can't I Change?

I came to understand the cycle of addiction a long time before I finally found freedom from my compulsive sexual behaviors. For me, understanding was never enough to break the strength of this self-reinforcing cycle. I desperately wanted to change, but understanding my enemy within was not enough for me, because I had a hidden piece in my cycle that would be found and disconnected only in a particular way. That reality is peculiar to my journey, and fortunately it's not true of most compulsive people. But make no mistake, change is hard, and simply understanding the addiction cycle alone is not enough for anyone to recover from addiction.

Unless you've been caught in this sort of compulsive vise, it's hard to understand why a person can't simply see the truth of how self-destructive his behavior is and just change it. The nature of addiction is that the chemical reinforcements released in the brain during addictive behavior reinforce the patterns of the addictive cycle. The chemically nurtured, feeling part of the brain is repeatedly strengthened and quickly develops the ability to overrule the reasoning part of the brain.

So, what does the addict need? Something greater than reasoning, something stronger than self-will and something more interventive than messages of shame or exhortation to make different choices. The addict needs truth and community, support and love, and the healthy reintegration of her life. This is where my story illustrates a difficult truth: way too often, the church is the last place an addict can find those things.

4

Shame and "Morality"

Surely he has borne our griefs
and carried our sorrows;
yet we esteemed him stricken,
smitten by God, and afflicted.
But he was pierced for our transgressions;
he was crushed for our iniquities;
upon him was the chastisement that brought us peace,
and with his wounds we are healed.
All we like sheep have gone astray;
we have turned—every one—to his own way;
and the LORD has laid on him
the iniquity of us all.

—THE PROPHET ISAIAH SPEAKING OF
THE SERVANT OF THE LORD (ISAIAH 53:4-6)

There is therefore now no condemnation
for those who are in Christ Jesus.

—PAUL TO THE CHURCH AT ROME (ROMANS 8:1)

I love our chocolate Labrador, Cashel, for lots of reasons. For instance, he's good company. One of the things I've noticed—

and this is true of lots of dogs—is that when he's being scolded, he looks like he's ashamed. But I don't think he is. His tail wags at the same time. I think that, like we do with other feelings, we project shame onto our dogs. The Creator seems to have gifted dogs with freedom from some of the things we as humans have to deal with, though we'd rather not. He has left shame and guilt to be burdens borne only by us humans.

Can Shame Be Good?

In the past few decades, many writers have tried to distinguish between good shame and bad shame, which I suppose might be understood as the difference between true guilt and false guilt. In *Shame and Grace*, Lewis Smedes wrote, "A healthy sense of shame is perhaps the surest sign of our divine origin and our human dignity. When we feel this sense of shame, we are feeling a nudge from our true selves."[1] He goes on to differentiate between healthy and unhealthy shame, and explains that unhealthy shame comes from our false self, that sense of our self we cobble together from negative sources.

In spite of many efforts to differentiate between true and false shame, or useful and negative shame, I believe we need to ditch the word *shame* altogether. The overarching connotations and impact of shame in our culture are so *dis*gracing that any helpful distinction about different "shames" can no longer be maintained. We've reached the point in the usage of the term *shame* that the distinction needs to be drawn between shame and true guilt, or healthy guilt.

It's absolutely essential to understand that, though shame gets confused with guilt, they are very different things. The confusion of the two makes spiritual growth and dealing with addiction harder. Guilt is the sense of remorse we have when we register a genuine discrepancy between what we ought to have done and what we actually have done. But what is shame? It is a powerful feeling, a strong emotion associated with guilt, embarrassment, unworthiness and disgrace.

When a person feels shame, he feels dishonored or disgraced or condemned. Living with a continuing feeling of being ashamed is being in a constant state of disgrace or dishonor. Shame and disgrace are linked; disgrace is a *dis*engaging from being in a state of grace. Shame is the absence of grace. In her book *Mindfulness and the 12 Steps,* Therese Jacobs-Stewart writes that shame is "a sense of being inherently deficient, indelibly stained."[2] Shame is something that should never be imposed on a child of God.

When we say "that's a shame" about an event that has befallen another, we mean *what happened* to the person is a disappointment. Whenever people feel shame, they are feeling *they* are the disappointment. In our culture, we've so often used *shame* to condemn others, we've rendered the term entirely toxic to spiritual and emotional health. A helpful distinction between shame and authentic guilt is made by Jacobs-Stewart: "Appropriate guilt occurs when we feel bad about a specific *behavior,* creating motivation for change. When shameful, on the other hand, we feel bad about *ourselves* after a specific event."[3] We need to let go of using the term *shame* and resolve to let go of the practice of shaming others.

Shame is toxic to strugglers. When we are broken people, when we are strugglers, we have a peculiar vulnerability to shame. We get the message that we are worthless, that in our brokenness we don't measure up to others' standards. We understand that there is something terribly wrong about us. But worse, for those of us who've stumbled into actively addictive lifestyles, shame is *toxic.* It fuels a miserable sense of self-loathing and makes life seemingly unbearable. Whether the source of our shaming is in our own heads or from others, shame makes the need for relief overwhelming. Shame in those of us with crippling dependencies makes our situation so difficult we are virtually incapable of breaking our cycles of self-abuse.

How Shame Is Used

What is shame used for and how does it work? The emotion of shame is intense and powerful. Our skin may feel hot and our faces turn red. We feel intense, personal pain. To get the pain to stop, we engage in efforts at self-control or self-moderation, modifying our behavior so as to avoid the pain of being shamed. Although shame can cause us to change our behavior, it rarely results in a truly good result, because even though we do exert some effort to control ourselves, we do it for the wrong reasons. What is worse, once we experience this dynamic and see the fruit of it, we begin to use shaming to control the behavior of others.

There are two reasons it is a very bad idea for us to use shame for modifying or controlling our behavior. First, even though shame can cause us to alter our behavior, at least for a while, we are not utilizing self-control out of love for ourselves or someone else. We are "changing" to stop the pain. We don't like how it feels to be ashamed, so we do what we can to stop the pain, but that is not a healthy motivation for changing our behavior. Why? Because we're responding to the message "I'm a worthless person" and hoping that by behaving differently we will no longer be worthless. We can stop the pain of false guilt, we think, by performing. It's trying to achieve a personal identity based on behavior and approval of others.

Now it's important we be clear that spiritual and emotional growth requires that we deal with true guilt. But dealing with true guilt is not the same as dealing with false guilt. False guilt is shame's sibling. It doesn't originate from healthy remorse over our behavior, but comes out of self-condemning and self-destructive images we have of ourselves. We have to learn to discriminate those voices in our self-reflection, to choose to listen to true remorse over what we've done and to reject those voices that condemn us as worthless and unloved persons.

We are all broken people in one way or another, and the way to healing is through dealing with our brokenness. But when the motivation and approach to behavior modification is to stop the pain by pleasing a demanding voice of accusation and self-worthlessness, the inner person is not healed, not forgiven, not made right with a new identity. The addict still perceives himself to be a worthless person making himself behave in a worthwhile way. But he is not changed.

Using shame to control others' behavior is also not good because it simply does not work in most instances. Years ago, an organization in our city tried to change the behavior of men visiting adult bookstores by utilizing the slogan "Real men don't use porn." It was a classic shaming technique. There was no noticeable decrease in adult-bookstore traffic (this was before the days of Internet porn), and after a while the campaign was discontinued.

I doubt that slogan helped anyone stop using porn. But I am sure it *did* make a lot of men feel worse about themselves. I imagine most men either struggled with the shame that slogan produced (I'm not a real man, then) or reacted in self-defense by defiantly rejecting the message. I felt particularly sensitive for my Christian brothers, struggling with self-shaming messages already, who saw those billboards and felt even worse about themselves. They felt worse, but were not empowered to healthy living.

This leads us to another reason to avoid shaming. Not only is shame ineffective in helping others or ourselves change our behavior, in some circumstances it actually reinforces the bad behavior. The idea of an addiction cycle, which we explored in the previous chapter, demonstrates how shaming actually reinforces the addict's need for relief.

Jesus and Shame

As the Master Physician of the human soul, Jesus never shamed people, including those who were sexually broken. He carefully handled people with honest truth, but never damning shame. He dealt in true guilt, and he valued personhood. The best portrayal of his attitude toward sexual brokenness and his approach to people with messy lives is his encounter with the woman at the well in John's Gospel (4:1-42).

Jesus and his small group of followers are making the journey from Judea in the south to Galilee in the north by passing through Samaria. Stopping at Jacob's Well, which is outside the town of Sychar, Jesus sends his disciples into the town to buy food while he rests alone at the well.

The encounter John relates occurs only because Jesus, while understood by John to be divine, is also human. As a real man, he experiences life as we experience it. After traveling eighty or so miles on foot over several days, he is tired and decides to rest at the well, which is outside of the town. And he is thirsty. The disciples go for his food; the woman draws for his drink. Known or unknown by us, God is with us in every aspect of our living, in every detail of our days. Jesus enters into our human experience in every way. He participates with us and he invites us to participate with him.

At about noon, a woman from the town comes out to draw water. This is not normal. Middle Eastern women draw water early in the morning and at dusk, and they always travel in groups.[4] What is it about this woman's life that she is going out to the well in the middle of the day and alone?

Normally Jews and Samaritans do not speak to each other, and women and men don't speak to each other either. Jesus breaks both of these social rules and asks the woman for a drink. Her response is to ask him how it is that he, a Jew, is asking her, a Samaritan, for a drink. She says it in a way that makes it clear she knows he's violating gender guidelines as well. She's intrigued by his social candor, but she's not put off by his behavior. Finding himself with a woman familiar with and at ease in the company of men, Jesus engages her in a life-changing conversation.

They have a fairly wide-ranging discussion on who he is, who the Jews are and what constitutes genuine worship. This woman may be having trouble taking this man seriously, but it's clear she enjoys sparring with him. Until it gets personal. Jesus tells her there is something about himself that she couldn't have guessed: though he is tired and thirsty, and though he needs her help to get water, he does have special powers. He can give her water to drink that will satisfy her beyond anything she's ever known. It is a different kind of water; it will fulfill her throughout her life. Even more intriguingly, this water he can give her will create an ongoing source within her own self that can satiate the thirst of others.

She thinks this Jewish man, while engaging and respectful, must be delusional. "Sir," she playfully retorts, "give me this water, so that I will not be thirsty or have to come here to draw water." He's been personal regarding himself and what he has to offer her; now he's about to get personal regarding her.

John tells us something in her response that is very important to catch. Jesus claims he can offer her two things: ending to her thirst and making her a resource to aid others.

Whether she is amused and entertained, and therefore only continuing the jousting, or she is now blown away by his bizarre claims, she picks up on the thing he can do *for* her, not the thing he can do *through* her. And in that, she is every woman and every man. When Jesus engages the woman at the well, he is engaging us. As Kenneth Bailey writes, we are all drawn to the kind of religion that satisfies ourselves.[5] But God draws us to himself both to be satisfied and to be of use to others.

At its heart, authentic Christianity is the exact opposite of compulsive living. The person struggling with compulsive behaviors is a prisoner to his own impulses and coping mechanisms, and so is neither satisfied nor available to others. As we learn to detach from our compulsions and attach ourselves to God, we increasingly experience contentment and usefulness to others. Unfortunately, this kind of authentic Christianity is not the experience that passes for Christianity for many Christians. For a lot of us, our practice and experience of the Christian faith is filtered through self-focus. While different from addiction, self-centered faith leaves us just as empty and just as unavailable to others.

So Jesus tells her to call her husband first. There's nothing playful in their interaction now; this woman has been married to five different men, none of whom are the man she's living with. She crisply responds, "I have no husband." And Jesus acknowledges that she's told the truth by telling her own history and present living arrangement. I think I'd be shut down by shame, but this woman surprises me. Hungry for things that matter, she recognizes there's no way this Jew could humanly know her story. He must be a man of God. Only God and her townspeople know her life. Jesus isn't from her social circle, so he has to be from God.

I don't think we can tell whether her next question is an at-

tempt to divert attention off her life or if she's got serious theological questions she's genuinely interested in clearing up. But
she says he must be a prophet, and what about the long-held
disagreement the Jews and Samaritans have had over the appropriate place to worship God? Jesus answers her question—note
how he takes her seriously—and then gives her a priceless piece
of instruction about what genuine worship is: God is interested
in people who worship him in "spirit and truth." And all of us
who care about the things of God and the genuine spiritual life
have to be grateful to her that she brought the issue up.

The upshot is that she then says something along the line of
this is all very interesting, and that even if she's not ready to buy
this Jew's opinion on the matter, she is confident that whether
Jew or Samaritan, the day will come when the Messiah appears
to both people and he'll clear all this mess up. Jesus absolutely
rocks the boat with his quietly thunderous, self-revealing
response: "I who speak to you am he." Life for this woman is
never going to be the same.

Just then the disciples return and are blown away that Jesus
is talking with a Samaritan woman. She returns to the town,
where she tells people that she met a man who displayed miraculous knowledge of her life; could this be the Prophet from
God (their code name for the Messiah or Christ)? Whatever we
might think her lifestyle had done to her reputation, the people
of her town listen to the woman. And they respond. They come
out to meet Jesus for themselves, and in their interaction with
him come to believe he is, indeed, the Messiah.

It's easy to miss that John gives us an astonishing piece of
information about the history of Christian preaching by including this story in his Gospel. He was writing later than the
other three Gospel writers and was clearly conscious of the fact
that God's move among humanity had expanded far beyond the

chosen people of Abraham's descendants to all races and all types of people. So perhaps we should not be surprised that it is John who tells us that the first preacher in Christian history, one personally acquainted with Christ himself, was a non-Jew, a woman and a person with significant sexual brokenness.

What does that tell us about Jesus, shame and compulsive sexual behavior? The thing that is really important to know about God is that he's never ever surprised by our failures, our brokenness. Nor is he put out by it, wringing his hands, or saying, "That's it. I'm done with him!" The person who in the eyes of heaven is the object of extravagant love and gentle tolerance may be very different from whom we might think. It may very well be that those who struggle with compulsive sexual behaviors are closer to the vulnerability and surrender the gospel demands than many others.

So shame is toxic to strugglers, is a lie about who we really are and is something Jesus refused to apply to those he came to set free. What is it about us that makes us so vulnerable to shame, and how does it get introduced into our self-destructive streams of consciousness?

Some of the Sources of Our Shame

First, the way others treat us is a key way in which we become vulnerable to shaming. If we've been abused, for instance, many of us develop the conviction that there is something about us that is abuse-worthy. Kids who suffer as their parents divorce often internalize the trauma by thinking their parents are divorcing because of something they did. If they'd been a better kid, or if they were worth sticking around for, then their parents wouldn't be splitting up.

Women, and some men, who are abused as children often find life partners who abuse them. This doesn't happen to everyone who's abused as a child; some become the abusers. But some of us have a particular vulnerability to the shame that victimization and pain cause, and we live our lives circling around the sewer of shame. The message we have for ourselves is that we're unworthy, we're damaged, we're bad, there's something wrong with us.

Second, our family system is the reason we get stuck in shame cycles and are vulnerable to the damage shaming does. In some of our families, we got the message—intentional or not—that we're not worth anything. It's intentional when an angry, abusive parent says things like, "Why did you do that? Can't you do anything right?" or "You're worthless." Other parents give a similar message, but without necessarily meaning to. They do it by ignoring us to the point we get the idea we're not worth their time or their attention.

In other families, some of us are emotionally and verbally abused by siblings who are allowed to carry on without correction from parents. Messages about our worth or lack of it, about how we never measure up or how we're an embarrassment to them—these and others damage our view of ourselves. We're shamed in the family system, and that shame becomes the overwhelming block to our ability to achieve an appropriate and healthy sense of who we are. That family system shame is a crushing threat to our well-being. It's more than we can handle, and we look for ways out whenever we feel the self-condemning feelings once we reach adulthood.

A third source of shame can be our own interior dialogue, the running subscript of our thinking that tracks in a downward spiral. Some of us have our own way of measuring ourselves as being insufficient people who are never good enough. We are literally our own worst enemies.

And finally, a source of shaming for many people—and this

is painful to write—is the church. I say it is painful to write because I love the church. Though it's true that a distinction exists between the genuine, authentic and spiritual followers of Jesus and the organization of Christianity as it's visibly constituted, that is a distinction only God has the right and ability to make. So I love the church. Another reason it pains me is that I have given the better part of my life to serving the church. And I have a cultivated humility—most of the time—that prevents me from judging the church. Yet we must be honest with what we know to be true. The church far too often shames people.

The church is such a huge, diverse entity, we're in danger of overgeneralization almost every time we form a statement about "the church does this" or "the church does that." Yet, for many folks, the very spiritual community where the message they ought to get is that they are unconditionally loved by God and God's people is a place of moralizing that ends up playing on their vulnerabilities to shame. Instead of love and redemption, the takeaway from Christian churches for far too many people is one of moralizing condemnation. They are told how they ought to behave in a spirit or style that condemns who they are.

Morality and Genuine Spirituality

It is the question of morality and genuine spirituality that brings us to the heart of the issue. *Morality* involves right and wrong conduct. A moral person is a person whose conduct is virtuous. When we moralize, we reflect on the behavior of ourselves, or more often on the behavior of others, and we pass moral judgments. In the church as many of us experience it today, emphasizing morality is an effort to control and conform behavior in ourselves and others to acceptable standards. It is an outer-focused, behavior-based way of measuring or evaluating the state of a person's mental, emotional and spiritual health. And it does not work.

If we see morality for what it is and understand its great limits, it can be somewhat useful. But when we confuse it with genuine spirituality and the worth of persons, it is flawed and even dangerous. Let me be clear: the issue is not whether or not our behavior matters. What we do with our lives matters greatly. It indicates something about the state of our hearts and the nature of our souls. Behavior matters. But we need to be extremely careful if we ever catch ourselves saying, "A Christian behaves in this way" or "A truly good person never does that." What could possibly be wrong with statements like this? Aren't Christians instructed by Jesus to be people who do not commit murder, for instance, or who take care of the poor? These are measurable behaviors. So, of course, how we live matters.

My issue with "morality" is the way in which we use it on ourselves and especially on others. It's not having moral standards that is the problem; it's the way we use them. We set up standards of behavior, and when people do not match them, we form judgments. We teach morality in such a way that we create lists of dos and don'ts, and then we evaluate. We judge—especially others—and as soon as we've done that, we've missed the whole point of healthy spirituality.

Nowhere in healthy living are we to be each other's judge. We measure the wrong things. We look at how a person lives, and we judge her by what we think her motives are. We look at a person's behavior, and we judge what we think is in his heart. When we don't measure up to "moral" standards, we are said to have "fallen" or "backslidden." We need to be "restored," because we no longer are part of the "moral" company of the church. Can this possibly be biblical Christianity?

This issue of morality and grace is slippery enough and confusing to so many of us that it's important to be very clear. Jesus instructs his followers that as they follow him, they will exhibit a righteousness more pure than that of the religious leaders of the day (see Matthew 5:20). Were that not a high enough goal, he tells us that all who are willing to be spiritually and behaviorally reformed by his word and God's Spirit will become completely integrated beings, even as God himself is a completely integrated being (see Matthew 5:48). It's not that the goal of becoming truly moral people is wrong; it's that the fruit of Christian moralizing does not bear the scent of the gospel but instead the stench of legalism.

Jesus sets the tone for how we are to approach behavior change (by grace and not by legalism) when he declares that it is a woeful practice to create heavy burdens for others to bear—burdens that those creating them cannot themselves bear (see Matthew 23:4-6). The woefulness is in behaviors that in and of themselves are not wrong and may even be right, but are not matched by the appropriate change within the person. Because the interior motivation must always be one of humility toward God and others, he says that God's desire is that we live by extending mercy and grace toward one another and avoiding any whiff of judgment (see Matthew 9:13).

The church has a troubling track record of lifting up one set of behaviors by giving them huge moral weight and ignoring other behaviors that are at least as or possibly more important. In many churches, "immoral" behavior is equated with sexual misconduct and abortion. These become the litmus tests for high morality. The question has to be asked, how did these two areas of moral behavior become the two most important? Jesus and the writers of Scripture call us to avoid gossip and gluttony, envy and greed, as well as other behaviors, but these are not only tolerated in "the church," they're actually exploited for the advantage of the institution.

A Genuinely Christian Morality

Our values over which behaviors indicate true morality are as skewed as our approach to each other is unchristian. Because of the way we judge each other, we become the evaluators of each other's spirituality and worth. This evaluation belongs to God alone. Read the Scriptures carefully, and you find that the pages of the Bible are filled with murderers and adulterers who love God and are loved by God. And a lot of their bad behavior seems to happen while they're in relationship with God. Could it be that God's way of approaching human morality and behavior is radically different from ours? I think so.

I think the subtle and convincing appeal of a moralizing approach to faith is this: if a person can live a dramatically self-sacrificing life or an apparently moral life, it is the curse of human nature to hear that whisper in our hearts, "I'm doing good things; I'm a moral person; God must be pleased with me." That is the whisper of spiritual idolatry. For instead of our love being focused on God and his desire to love us in spite of ourselves, it's focused on us and our achievements. Jesus calls us to do what we do and to want to do what he wants us to do only because we are increasingly captivated by God's passionate love for us.

Are some behaviors more morally essential than others? Are some teachings of Jesus to be elevated over others? When Jesus sketched for his disciples what it might look like when the Great Evaluation is held in the life to come, his notions were that feeding the hungry and visiting prisoners would be much more important than serving in church leadership or giving to church building campaigns. Somewhere, and often, we've gotten far away from the genuine gospel. And we've done it because it's easier for most of us to truncate the gospel into a small set of behaviors. It's too messy and too demanding to let go of everything we hold dear and follow

Jesus. Why? Because none of us do it very well. We all fail. And when we fail, we need mercy—the pity of God. And needing God's pity puts us all on the same footing.

The dark side of Christian morality is that some of us so want to feel good about ourselves that we convince ourselves God is probably pretty glad we're on his side. We wouldn't say that out loud; maybe we don't even recognize we're thinking it. But scratch beneath our moral hypocrisy, and you find the notion that we think we're a good catch for the side of heaven. When we finally confront that attitude for what it is, it appalls us.

Some of us need to feel good about ourselves at the expense of others. And some of us really have too much pride to be pitiful before God. That's at the heart of it, I think, our pride. When we're addicts, our pride has to be served to cover up the disordered mess inside. We shortcut; we act out; we are selfish, hurtful people. But when we start to face up to who we really are, pride has to go. For the genuinely honest person who struggles with compulsive sexual behaviors, there is no pride to cling to, no sense of personal morality to hide behind. It's all stripped away, and we are pitiful people, folks who know we need mercy or we haven't got a prayer.

So honesty with myself, with God and with others is absolutely essential if I'm going to successfully deal with my compulsive nature and behaviors. Truth opens me to genuine humility and letting go of pride. But with whom do I disclose and how much? How much of my story do you need to know? How much of my story do I need to tell you to be clear that I'm being genuinely honest with myself?

Appropriate Disclosure

It's natural to be curious, and even if we're not consciously aware of it, most of us are intrigued to know what others have done. As you read this book, you may very well think things like, *Tom isn't saying much about the actual behaviors he's engaged in over the years*, or *I wonder what specific things Tom has been tempted with*. When I began to attend a Twelve Step recovery group, the protocol was to avoid excessive detail. Whether details in sharing are pornographic or distract others by leading them to be excited or to judge the behavior, they are not the point, never helpful and sometimes damaging.

I am a sexually broken person who struggled for forty years with a deeply entrenched addiction to lust and pornography. While it is the nature of addiction to be progressive, my faith warred against my addiction in such a way that my compulsive behaviors certainly did not progress to all the expressions they might have. It was a veritable war in my soul, and war is messy. My accountability circle has helped shape my approach to telling my story by being repeatedly clear that it is important and healthy that we all be restrained and disciplined regarding detailed behavioral disclosures. I'm clearly saying that I'm a sexually broken person, it cost me dearly, and Jesus has helped me and will help you too.

The goal of life change isn't a clean slate, a stunning turnaround in behavior or an attainment of the approval of others. *The goal of life change is the genuine integration of God's presence and ways with a person's values and behaviors.* That integration results in the healing of our soul and life, so that we are increasingly able to connect well with our self, with our Creator and with others. So if it's integration and soul care we're about, it's important for all of us to exercise self-restraint in disclosure of specific behaviors.

There are three reasons for this restraint. First, some spheres of self-disclosure are necessary to healing but are specific to proximity. I owe my wife a much fuller accounting than my friends; my sponsor gets a much more detailed inventory than group members; my children hear more than the board of my former church; and so on. So, what do people need to know about my journey beyond the facts that I was broken, that sexual brokenness was the primary symptom of deeper issues and that I suffered significant consequences as a result of my choices?

Second, both in the culture at large and in the church, we rank sins, and when a self-discloser gets into details, the scoring begins. It's not biblical, helpful or wise. It does not foster anything positive. It's unhelpful for the discloser and a temptation to rank sin for everyone else.

Third, we need to change the way we think about and approach sexual brokenness in people, and so we must recalibrate our approach to it with an absence of judging. It's essential, then, that we model coming forward with an admission like mine, not going into confession of specific behaviors. We don't expect detailed confessions about anyone else's self-harming and other-harming behaviors (gluttony, gossip, idol worship, to name a few), so why do we make sexual sins different from others? It becomes prurient for people to be told or want to know too much.

What does a genuinely remorseful person need to tell about his brokenness? Only what is necessary to make the appropriate amends to specific people, and no more. To a priest, a sponsor or an old and trusted friend—so that we're experiencing genuine connecting with another—we tell everything. But to everyone else? There are circles of disclosure, and most people are in the outer rings.

We are in danger of creating a second class of citizens in the society of Jesus' followers. The shaming of sexual brokenness is so palpable in most churches that those of us who are guilty of having a struggle with sexual brokenness feel we don't really belong. Could this possibly be what Jesus wants?

It's the rest of us who are *not* addicts who may be in the biggest spiritual trouble. Because we've not bottomed out, our behaviors aren't as obviously destructive. We're more "moral," and that's dangerous, because wherever human beings have a personal sense of being moral, pride grows like mushrooms on a dung heap.

It's sometimes said that the ground at the foot of the cross is level. That means all of us are on the same footing; all of us are in need of grace, in need of pity. All of us need to be loved. We try to find those things in various ways, but shame and "moral" living are two ways that don't work.

Excavating Origins

When I was eight, the imposter, or false self, was born as a defense against pain. The impostor within whispered, "Brennan, don't ever be your real self anymore because nobody likes you as you are. Invent a new self that everybody will admire and nobody will know." So I became a good boy—polite, well-mannered, unobtrusive, and deferential. I studied hard, scored excellent grades, won a scholarship in high school, and was stalked every waking moment by the terror of abandonment and the sense that nobody was there for me.

—BRENNAN MANNING, *ABBA'S CHILD*

It's increasingly clear to me that God does not waste things. Somehow, in the marvelous and mysterious way in which he interacts with his creation, everything matters. The smallest details and the most insignificant aspects of our lives are not lost in the way in which God weaves our history with his unfolding drama. Jesus tips us off to this dynamic in God's ways when he cautions us that the Almighty notices every bird that falls from the sky and knows the number of hairs on each human head.

So it should come as no surprise that no matter how crazy or demeaning our life becomes, the unraveling of all the past is instrumental in structuring a healthier future. I understand the cry to "just move on" and "let the past go." Most of us are familiar with folks who are stuck in the past, who keep rehearsing hurts they've suffered and pieces of their history. There is a tension here because, for some of us, trying to focus on life now and letting go of the past does not work. Instead, it creates a logjam of debris in our soul. Avoiding or not successfully resolving a piece of our past can rob us of the ability to find peace, joy and contentment in the present.

I learned a great deal about addiction, and I genuinely worked at recovery, but no matter how much I practiced the recovery principles in all the aspects of my life, I couldn't move very far forward. I was stuck. I would make progress, yes. I was growing slowly. But something kept pulling at me and tripping me up. For reasons I could not identify, I kept relapsing. Why?

Now, every person's story is different; every life has its own nuances. For a lot of people, the basic work of methodically going back over their life and doing a thorough inventory (usually with the help of a guide) provides the insights necessary to recognize what needs to be confronted, discarded or addressed by amends. To some degree, all who want to deal with compulsive behaviors have to do the very hard and threatening work of excavating, identifying, resolving and releasing the critical elements of their own stories. For some of us, however, it turns out that a bit more will be required. That was true of me.

My Wiring and an Unhelpful Environment

I came into the world a relatively intelligent boy. For reasons well beyond my capability to understand, I was assembled pre-delivery with a number of features that weren't particularly special or debilitating, but as my postdelivery life unfolded, each of them played a significant part in the way in which I would struggle in the world. I had a personality prone to meet stress and stimulation in life with anxiety. I had attention deficit hyperactivity disorder. I was sensitive, and I was mildly obsessive-compulsive.

In other words, I was an ordinary boy, full of promise and life with a few challenges, but nothing that couldn't be dealt with in the right environment.

It's an understatement to say the immediate family into which I was born was as unhelpful and hurtful in regard to what I needed as any family could be. My father, a gentle and nice man, was overmatched by life. It's clear now (but was unrecognized then) that he suffered a form of Asperger's syndrome, a disorder characterized by limitations in certain social and linguistic skills. He never once expressed any of his feelings for me or what he thought about me until late in his life, when he managed to pen the words "I'm proud of you" onto a Christmas card. Until then, the only notion I had that I was special to my father came from others who didn't hear it from him either, but were sure it was true.

We didn't talk. Not about anything. Ever. When I was young, he had two jobs: one as a bookkeeper for a brokerage firm and a second as a ticket taker at the professional ballpark in our town. Sometimes—when my mother told him to—he took me along to the ballpark. In those days, security wasn't what it is now, and while he was working, I'd wander around the place. But when he was done counting the ticket stubs, he and I would retreat together to the standing-room-only portion of the stadium and watch the remainder of the game.

Looking back, I can see that my father was probably obsessed with baseball. He always held his handheld transistor radio up to his ear when ball games were being broadcast, until the day he got an earplug and could put the radio elsewhere. So at the ballpark, there we would be, father and son: father watching the game and listening to his radio, son bored out of his mind. He never spoke to me of baseball. Frankly, I didn't understand the game.

I think it must have been terribly disappointing for him— but again, it's hard to know for sure—that when my mother enrolled me in the local Little League team and I had my one season at playing the sport, I was abysmal. I clearly remember my ill-fitting and scratchy uniform and my display of futility at the plate. Three swings and I would gratefully retreat back to the bench. Had I actually ever hit the ball, I'm not sure I would have known where to run. Or why.

But here's the point: it wasn't until after he was dead that I learned from my youngest cousin that my dad knew every statistic there was to know in baseball. Matt was home from school one summer, and my dad—having a particularly rough patch in making his life work—was living with Matt's folks, Dad's youngest sister and brother-in-law. Matt and my dad spent hours watching baseball on TV. Matt would comment about this player's stats or wonder out loud about the season that player was having, and if he waited, my father would cough, clear his throat hesitantly and recite the player's entire career statistics.

Amazing. I think he knew everything there was to know about baseball, and we never played catch. I can't identify like a lot of other men can with Kevin Costner's *Field of Dreams* character, but I still choke up in the closing scene when Costner's Ray Kinsella plays catch with his dad.

I wrote earlier that we have to learn to excavate, identify and then resolve and release the essential elements of our upbringing, and I've done that with my father. He was a good man totally overmatched by life. He died living alone in a subsidized studio apartment with no phone or checking account. He worked at the night desk of a downtown hotel. When I wanted to reach him, I had to call him there while he was on duty or leave a note on his apartment door. I saw him when I made the effort.

Left to himself, I would hear from him around Christmas most every year (one year he even missed Christmas). I believe he loved me. But the pieces I had to excavate and identify, resolve and release were connected to the fact that having him as my father was like being abandoned, only without it being obvious. He was sort of in my life, but not really. He was like a ghost.

My mother was a very different story. Restless, envious and incapable of finding contentment, she grew up the middle of five love-starved children. Her father was an athletic, charming storyteller and womanizer. He was horribly undependable, disappearing after getting in arguments with her mother and finally abandoning his wife and five children in the midst of the Great Depression. Her mother was dramatic and high strung, almost certainly bipolar and misunderstood by all except her own late father, Thomas Clayton (a Methodist preacher after whom my mother named me), who died when she was young. My mother's life growing up was a perfect storm of insanity, chaos and abandonment, one that she recreated for me.

Like her mother, she was bipolar and untreated. I'm not bipolar, but I learned to live that way under her overwhelming tutelage. As flat as my father was, my mother was full. She dominated my life the way the Earth dominates the moon. Only more so.

Don't assume from what I'm writing that I'm blaming my life on my mother. My life is my life, and my problems are my responsibilities to deal with. But excavating a life brings up facts, and as one of our recent presidents famously observed, facts can be devilishly stubborn things to deal with. The facts are that my mother was sick and unhappy. She married a man who she was sure would be successful in a white-collar career, but not ambitious when it came to other women. My father's work as a bookkeeper was not successful, and their marriage was a disaster.

Looking back over the wreck of our lives together, I can't imagine two people more ill-suited for one another. Our home wasn't just unhappy, it was menacingly dark. My mother—out of her illness and psychotic need to find deliverance in the one child she was willing to bear—ladled manic praise over and about me when she was up and abused me abysmally when she was down.

And for a very long time, I thought my house was like every other kid's.

My Four Coping Mechanisms

Coming into this maelstrom of emotional chaos with an oversensitive set of wires, I was set up for disaster. But I was intelligent and I was a survivor, so I found a way through it. I did what a bazillion other kids have done in similarly abusive situations: I learned to dissociate. What I could not have known or understood then, but have since learned, was that in dissociating, I was set up for the psychobiological development of becoming a sexually compulsive person.

I learned how to unplug the searing heat of pain and craziness in my little world by emotionally separating myself. I learned to break away from the insanity and mercurial threats by doing four things. I could *disappear.* Hide. Just be somewhere else from where the heat and fire were. I could *deceive.* "No, Mommy, I don't know anything about that." "No, Mommy, I didn't see that." "No, Mommy, that's not what they said." The third thing I learned in life was that I could *eat* to feel better sometimes. Sneaking certain things and putting things like cookies in my mouth made me feel better inside whenever my external reality was dishing up things that made me feel awful. I was now well on my way to a lifestyle of mood alteration. It worked, even if it wasn't healthy. But these three behaviors paled in comparison to what I found next.

When I entered adolescence, I discovered the most intoxicating and destructive dissociative technique of all: *lust and masturbation.* I didn't have older brothers or close friends to teach me, so I stumbled on the whole sex thing clumsily. But I was a fast learner. I couldn't possibly know then what I know now: that sexual arousal begins a dopamine drip in the brain that culminates in a chemical blowout with orgasm. And I wasn't socially secure or popular with other kids, so all my sexual acting out was in my head. But I was an intelligent kid and could put my mind and what scraps of underwear ads I could find to use. I cultivated a world of fantasy where I was in charge for the first time, where things happened as I desired them and where I was always the one desired, the one taken care of.

I became a dopamine and adrenaline junky. By the time I was leaving adolescence for adulthood, I was an addict. I had no idea I was an addict. But the four skills I'd acquired to handle my life were not left behind in my high-school locker. I headed off to college with next to no ability to handle my emotions in healthy ways, but with excellently honed skills in disappearing, deceiving, using food for mood elevation and using lust and eventually porn to keep myself moving forward.

My Inability to Attach Healthily

If my four coping mechanisms were the *psychobiological* setup for my compulsive sexual behaviors, I unfortunately had a *psy-*

chosocial dynamic at play too. This is very important to understand for anyone who is in relationship with or attempting to
help people suffering with compulsive behaviors like mine.

When we refer to someone as being an addict, we mean that
she lives in "a state of compulsion, obsession or preoccupation"[1]
that makes it impossible for her to exercise her will and desire
in a free way. She is compelled by her interior thinking/feeling
processes to seek relief from stress, anxiety and boredom by
using her addictive (compulsive) behavior. Being addicted
means her energy and her deepest desires to be a person who
loves and who has integrity get sidetracked. The origin of this
state is the sidetracking of the addict's ability to attach to other
people in healthy relationships. Instead she becomes attached
to unhealthy behaviors to meet the needs that healthy relationships were intended to meet. "Attachment, then, is the process
that enslaves desire and creates the state of addiction," Gerald
May writes.[2]

Because of the deficiencies that plagued both of my parents, I
was unable to attach—that is, to find the security every human
child needs. All of us need to find security, comfort, pleasure
and soothing in the context of a safe, nurturing relationship.
Instead, I found neglect and abandonment on the one hand and
threatening chaos, emotional smothering and more abandonment on the other. Again, I'm not blaming my parents for
my life or for what are my responsibilities. But the reality is that
I didn't find safety and security in my upbringing, characterized
by the acceptance, soothing and comfort that would have allowed me to learn how to form healthy emotional relationships.
Instead, the threat of loss, abandonment and chaos kept me
fractured emotionally and unable to bond in healthy ways.

What does an attachment deficit have to do with developing
compulsive sexual behaviors? A 1999 study indicated that 95

percent of sexually compulsive people have insecure, or dysfunctional, attachment styles.[3] When I discovered the (mis)use of my own sexuality, I found a replacement for lack of healthy attachment. When I was attracted to certain images and fantasies, fueled by my emerging sexual development, those images and fantasies inadvertently became surrogates seemingly offering me the comfort and acceptance I'd not been given in real life. This is why we say that those struggling with compulsive sexual behaviors are suffering from intimacy woundedness or an intimacy deficit.

Frankly, with both psychobiological issues and psychosocial issues, there was no way I was going to live to adulthood without becoming a sex addict.

Lies I Learned

All of us have some baggage from our upbringing that we need to sort through. Some of us have a little stuff we need to toss, but most of the rest of what we got we can rearrange and re-outfit—and we do all right with it. Others of us need to do some major dumpster donations from our childhood. I found at least seven forms of distorted thinking I acquired in the psychological enmeshment I had with my mother. None of these were clearly stated, but they were communicated forcefully, and they informed and guided me all the way into my fifties. Until I successfully unplugged myself from performing and from her, and could get to the core of what was mixing around in my sub-soul, those seven lies, outlined below, confounded my spirituality and my attempts to recover from compulsive sexual behavior.

We know better. Through constant repetition and convincing demonstration, I learned that if we feel strongly about something, then no matter what someone else thinks, our feeling is right. Now, we might agree with someone while in their presence and nod our head like we're agreeing, but later we remark what nonsense it is. Where does such an unhealthy and untrue life perspective come from? I think its origins come from distrust of others because of abandonment and deep insecurity. These are expressed through the emotions of bitterness and envy.

We must be great. Many addicts suffer from a need to perform, a sort of grandiosity that we can overperform and compensate for the failures we are. I got a head start in grandiose thinking because early on I learned that I must be exceptional. While I couldn't have recognized it at the time, being exceptional was what my mother desperately needed me to be. Simply being good or right was not enough.

I think a lot of people in professional ministry, like all caregiving professions, are motivated by a need to be needed. But I didn't understand until many years later how absolutely shackled I was to the need to perform, and it was a hindrance to my recovery. Because of who I was and how I grew up, it was essential that people be "wowed" when they encountered me and that they talk later about how exceptional I was. Why? The significance, justification and vindication of my family system were all at stake. And the cruel irony was that no matter how good I was, nothing I accomplished would ever be enough.

We are special. This guiding principle wasn't so subtle. I developed a deep sense of this from early days. The mythical stories of my miraculous conception and death-defying birth; the oft-repeated railings of how difficult life was; the vaguely expressed notion that no one really understood us and our suffering, but someday they would—all these and more underlined the notion that our life was very, very tragic and yet, because of who I would become, all the more special.

We must hide. I learned that there are things about our lives that no one needs to know. In fact, it's important for our well-being that no one knows certain things. A family member helped support us by giving my mother money monthly, and this went on for years. We must have gotten thousands and thousands of dollars, but no one else in the family was to know. I became dimly aware of the money somehow. One of my aunts must have become aware of it, too, but my mother wouldn't own up to it. There were many secrets about our life; keeping others from knowing everything was to our advantage.

We don't have to be honest. Many, many times I heard something expressed that I knew was not what we really thought. I learned the skillful survival art of shading things, of telling part of a story so that it created a certain impression and of avoiding anything that may paint us in an unfavorable light or be a disadvantage. The point was to create the right impression for others so that they would think in ways that were favorable to us. It was how we could protect ourselves and get from others what we wanted. Growing up this way, I became a deceiver and a liar.

We recruit others to rescue us. This was how we survived, so I didn't learn to become self-sufficient. I'm embarrassed now as I look back on my life that I didn't learn how to work hard or to be a self-starter. I've learned those things now, but I didn't learn them when I should have. I had to overcome the pernicious thinking that if we could work others' feelings and sympathies—and you had to learn how to read others to do this—then we could enlist their help and they would take care of us. I learned this practice well and often used it.

If we think something's wrong with us, we will fix it—no one else. This lie came partly from the idea that we were the only ones we could trust to decide if there really was something wrong with us. We and we alone. Related to this was the idea that we could not possibly become genuinely intimate with anyone else. Intimacy with another person meant allowing someone else to know something that might give them control over us; and life taught us that was not allowable. Only embarrassment and hurt and pain could come from that. We could not be open. We could not be vulnerable. In this area, if only this area, we relied only on ourselves. No one else.

As I reflect on these seven lies, there is one other significant lie I learned growing up and one essential truth I've learned since. The additional lie is that *joy isn't real.* There is no real joy, only pretend joy. There is anticipation of real joy, but no real joy. I can see now that we looked to external sources for relief—really distraction—from prevailing moods. Whether it was the celebration of a holiday or the visit of a relative, the anticipation was that something really good was going to happen, life would be good and we would be happy. But it always ended empty and joyless. As an addict—even one deep into recovery—it's sometimes hard to believe in joy.

Though I learned these lies while living with my mother, who acquired them herself through a combination of mental illness, deprivation and abandonment, they became truly mine. I am the one who lived them. Their ongoing existence in my thinking was my responsibility—no one else's—and confronting them and replacing them with truth was my responsibility too. I suspect most people who struggle with compulsive sexual behaviors, as well as most other addicts, recognize a lot of their own stories in these lies I learned. An important part of growing up and becoming a healthy adult is reparenting ourselves.

What I Didn't Learn but Really Needed To

If a kid has about half of a decent parenting team—and this can be cobbled together between two parents, stepparents or a neighbor or friend's parent—he can learn how to do basic things that give him what he needs to grow up to be relatively healthy. Hopefully he can put together the rest with coaches, teachers, mentors, books, friends, a spouse and other sources of insight.

One of the key lessons to be learned is how to manage our feelings, or how to handle emotion regulation. When we're high, how do we modify ourselves and not fly out the upstairs window? When we're low, how do we deal with disappointment and not bottom out? I didn't learn any of that. I learned dissociation.

One of the elements of my life that made things interesting was that I was a stealth emotion-nonregulator. You would never have noticed it. I was an only child, so I learned how to deal with adults, how to speak to them. I was privileged to attend good public schools, so I picked up some relatively healthy socializing techniques there. I was a nerd and socially awkward, so I didn't move with the popular kids. That meant I never learned to drink or do drugs. This happened to be a really good thing. My therapist told me years later that kids with my combination of personal wiring and home environment typically become drug addicts and die by age twenty-five through overdose or suicide. Not me. Never did drugs (other than sexual fantasy-induced dopamine and adrenaline).

The other upside, I suppose, to being such a nerdy kid was that I didn't acquire the social skills or have the self-confidence to date girls. That meant that all my sexual escaping was alone. But it also meant I lived too much in my head. And that just wasn't a good place to be, because I *needed* to be special. I was driven. I was a relatively successful, adult-pleasing, high-functioning head case.

There was one other important formative aspect to my upbringing: we went to church. Church was a big part of our fam-

ily's life, but we weren't the kind of people who talked about
Jesus or even about the minister's sermon. My mother would
comment on the music in the service or that it was nice to see
so-and-so back from wherever they'd been. It was important for
her to have contact with the minister or his wife, because this
made her feel important. We went to a Presbyterian church,
and I've since figured out that this was important to my mother.
All her family was Methodist. But when her oldest sister re-
belled by bolting to the Presbyterians, my mother followed.
Out of her need for significance, she wanted to be where she
thought the higher class people were.

The thing about going to Sunday school and church every
week and youth group and summer youth camp was this: I developed a God-consciousness. I was squirrely and distracted,
though I always was well-behaved sitting next to my mother in
church (fear and anxiety can shape a person), but along the way
I acquired my own distinctive understanding that there is a
God and He Is Really Important. I even had a few times when I
felt the actual nudge of the Holy Spirit in my consciousness.

A Genuine, Rock-Solid Spirituality

As I mentioned earlier, during high school I went to the youth
ministry of a different church, and there my spirituality was
ignited into a full-blown, personal pursuit of Jesus of Nazareth. I
can still remember the night in June of 1972, sitting on the floor
of a dingy old house in which the youth ministry met, sun
streaming through the old elm trees to the west of the picture
window, a red-haired guitarist strumming "He's Everything to
Me" and "Pass It On." I thought, *These people are living and feeling
what I've always believed in. This is for me.* And I never looked back.

Having my faith take form did two things to my life as a
struggler with compulsive sexual behaviors. On the one hand,

my growing personal involvement with Jesus and others trying to follow him served to restrain the natural trajectory of my addiction. Again, addiction is a progressive disease; it doesn't allow a person to plateau. Its destructive power feeds on incremental advancement: what serves as a shortcut today won't serve the same way tomorrow. More of the "drug" is needed. Addiction is the monster that demands more. But my faith warred against my addiction and kept me from progressing to where I might have gone.

On the other hand, my faith reinforced my guilt and my shame. I figured out pretty quickly that it wasn't okay to practice the Christian faith and lust over every attractive girl in my Bible study. So I tried to stop self-gratifying. I promised myself I would stop masturbating. I promised God I wouldn't engage in any of these disappointing behaviors anymore. I seriously meant it.

And I couldn't stop.

One time I talked with my Bible study leader, haltingly of course. I told him I had this problem, this thing I shouldn't be doing. I didn't seem to be able to stop. Did he know of anything I could read about it? When he figured out what I was talking about, he turned beet red. This wasn't his fault; it's just that we didn't talk about these things. He didn't have anything I could read. He didn't have anything to say. When I heard his words and saw how his face became red—he's a really, really good guy, his reaction wasn't his fault—I thought, *Oh, this is something you don't talk about. You fix this on your own.* I knew all about living life on your own, so it made sense.

Like so many of us back then, I figured when I got married and started having sex with my wife, my problem would go away. When my problem came back a few months into our marriage, my shock and dismay were crippling. I felt sick. By then I was heading toward seminary and ministry. People thought I had something to offer the church, but I had this problem, and I wasn't sure what I was going to do about it. I was confused, ashamed and scared. What was wrong with me? The intimacy I enjoyed with my wife was very good, and yet I would still return to the same old behaviors.

I heard about a Christian counselor—this was relatively unknown in our circles back in the seventies—at another church in a different part of town. He was kind and understanding. But when I described my struggle, just like my Bible-study leader, he turned crimson. He said it would take a lot of sessions and we'd need to talk about my parents and other things in my background. I didn't have any money for a lot of counseling sessions. But worse than that, I could tell by his reaction that he was embarrassed by me and my behavior. Between the financial cost and the shame cost, I was out of there. I'd have to fix this on my own.

At no point did I ever think, *Well, this just isn't a big deal,* about my sexual struggles. Or, *I'm gifted in other ways; this is just something I need on the side and it doesn't matter.* Even then my faith was holistic: I knew that what we do with our bodies comes out of what's going on in our souls and spirits. Behavior *does* matter.

So, though I struggled with my behaviors and kept trying to stop, my need for my "drug" to survive, to manage my ups and downs, was locked into my soul. The addiction warred with my faith, demanding my acquiescence, my surrender. My faith warred with my compulsive behaviors, demanding that Jesus and his gospel have all of me. Hypocrisy would not be tolerated; whole obedience was required. Addiction fought faith, and faith fought addiction. These forces waged war on the battlefield of my soul and it would take a long time and a lot of effort before one triumphed over the other.

6

Genuine Spiritual Transformation and the Recovery Movement

Brothers, if anyone is caught in any transgression,
you who are spiritual should restore him in a spirit of gentleness.
Keep watch on yourself, lest you too be tempted.
Bear one another's burdens, and so fulfill the law of Christ.

—Paul to the Galatians (Galatians 6:1-2)

If it seems presumptuous for a survivor of a long struggle in the wilderness of compulsive living to have thoughts about what makes for genuine spiritual transformation and authentic spiritual community, I agree with you. On the other hand, I suppose those of us who have longingly looked through the prison bars of our compulsivity at the freedom others seemingly enjoy have earned the right to think insightfully about these things. And if we've really struggled with ourselves and worked at recovery, we actually have some useful thoughts to offer on the subject. So it's with a spirit of genuine humility and sincere desire for transformation that I offer this chapter.

I did work very hard and for a long time at my recovery

before experiencing the sustained sobriety and growing serenity I longed for. I struggled a good deal to overcome my intimacy woundedness by working at my interpersonal relationships. I had two sponsors and worked with two therapists. I attended sex-addiction recovery groups, and I began a confidential one for clergy. My desire for personal transformation motivated a lot of what I did in ministry. So in the process of learning a great deal about recovery and spiritual transformation, I discovered how important being part of a healthy community is for genuine life change.

Further, I came to understand that recovery from addiction—any addiction or compulsive behavior or the codependent compulsions so many of us struggle with—is a subcategory of spiritual transformation. People in the recovery movement are taught that recovery is spiritual in nature. They benefit by drawing on Christian spiritual practices as tools for their recovery. Folks in the church need to understand that genuine recovery is not necessarily different from or opposed to Christian spiritual transformation. The big challenge human beings face is becoming aware of who we are and how we behave—and not settling for being less than a whole, healthy person. To be healthy, spiritual people, we all need to change, so what does that look like?

What Is Spiritual Transformation?

The beginning of genuine transformation is the recognition of brokenness. Addicts know pain. That's why we're addicts—we've found ways of shortcutting personal pain so we don't have to feel. The shortcuts have sculpted highways in our brains so that in the miasma of muddling through life, whenever we're too high, too low, afraid, threatened or bored, our autodrive takes over and we're gone. Addicts know pain. Pain upon pain. Discouragement—the absence of encouragement, the absence of being able to muster personal courage to face what needs facing.

It isn't only addicts who are broken, though. All of us are. In some ways we can understand that every daughter of Eve and son of Adam is a person with a flawed nature, someone who attaches to people and things instead of God and who often struggles with not doing the right thing. We all mess up; we all go astray; we all are selfish. We all are broken. Recognizing this is the beginning of change. Out of the floodwaters of chaos comes the drying of a new day. God is putting the broken world and the broken people in it back together again. Spiritual transformation is part of that work. It's useful to the processes of transformation to recognize our brokenness and to seek God's help in finding our way to wholeness.

Another way of thinking about spiritual brokenness is that we have divided hearts. Unless we are sociopathic, none of us has an entirely darkened or destructive heart. But none of us has an entirely good heart either. This is what every human being has in common with people who are addicts: we all suffer from having divided hearts and therefore divided actions. We make decisions and we sculpt our lives based on what is going on in our hearts. "Actions are not impositions on who we are, but are expressions of who we are," Dallas Willard writes. "They come out of our heart and the inner realities it supervises and interacts with."[1]

There are techniques of life change we can discover and employ. For instance, when I decided that I simply could not manage my recovery if I continued to allow myself the opportunity to view Internet pornography on my computer without accountability, I installed a brilliant software program that reports each week to my three accountability partners each and every website my computer goes to.[2] I've not looked at Internet pornography since. Not once. The technique of managing that aspect of my behavior worked, and so it was very helpful toward achieving real transformation. Practical strategies are important, but alone they are not enough.

Because the heart must change.

So how do we change our hearts? As we've already seen, we have to recognize our brokenness. If the addict is the "extreme example of self-will run riot," as AA's Big Book says,[3] then this recognition of brokenness is timelessly expressed in step one of the Twelve Steps: We admitted we were powerless over our compulsive sexual behavior (or powerless over our selfishness, our anger, our laziness, our judgmentalism, our *brokenness*) and that our lives had become unmanageable.[4]

The Twelve Steps unfold as a short course in personal transformation and are effective if they're truly worked as a lifelong program of learning and doing. The rest of the steps are as follows:

- Step two: Came to believe that a Power greater than ourselves could restore us to sanity.

- Step three: Turned our will and our lives over to the care of God, as we understood God.

- Step four: Made a searching and fearless moral inventory of ourselves.

- Step five: Admitted to God, to ourselves, and to another human being the exact nature of our wrongs.

- Step six: Were entirely ready to have God remove all these defects of character.

- Step seven: Humbly asked him to remove our shortcomings.

- Step eight: Made a list of all persons we had harmed, and became willing to make amends to them all.

- Step nine: Made direct amends to such people wherever possible, except when to do so would injure them or others.

- Step ten: Continued to take personal inventory and when we were wrong promptly admitted it.

- Step eleven: Sought through prayer and meditation to improve our conscious contact with God as we understood him, praying only for knowledge of his will for us and the power to carry that out.

- Step twelve: Having had a spiritual awakening as the result of these steps, we tried to carry this message to other addicts, and to practice these principles in all areas of our lives.

The Twelve Steps and the Church

For thousands and thousands of folks, the Twelve Steps have proven to be a very useful tool for helping them overcome compulsive behaviors. An obvious issue—and one many Christians cite as a concern about the veracity of the Twelve Steps—is how the concept of God is expressed as a lowest-common-denominator "Higher Power." Christian thinking and teaching clearly understands God as much more self-defined, the personally revealing mysterious Being with a trinitarian nature. It might be useful to point out that many American Christians seem to have a functional faith that settles for an innocuous deity more in line with the Higher Power of the recovery movement. Most people sitting in American churches today live as functional agnostics—and I include the conservative part of the church in that assessment. But the question before us is, can Christians utilize the Twelve Steps with their understanding of who God is, and can the Twelve Steps be used in a Christian setting?

The recovery movement, of which I'd say Alcoholics Anonymous—both the organization and the book (which contains the original Twelve Steps)—is the fundamental cornerstone, is pitched to a broad-based culture as a necessity. The brilliance of the movement, proven by it's multicultural effectiveness, is that it makes the whole concept of a divine being as accessible as possible, while keeping a foot in the door of faith for those who'd most likely ignore it but for their desperate need for a solution to their problem. Therefore, to reach as many people as possible with the message that there is hope for the hopelessly addicted, it was prudent for the founders to refer to the divine being as the Higher Power rather than other names by which we know God.

It's clear when you read *Alcoholics Anonymous* that Bill Wilson had a personal and significant life encounter with Jesus Christ. It's also very clear in chapter four, "We Agnostics," that Wilson and the founders of the movement felt that faith in God made sense if only a person was open to it. "Deep down in every man, woman and child, is the fundamental idea of God" and "Some of us grow into it [faith] more slowly. But He has come to all who have honestly sought Him."[5] The Twelve Steps themselves have a biblical basis historically. Wilson and the other founders of the movement drew on the teachings of the Oxford movement, a nineteenth-century renewal effort in the Anglican Church in Great Britain that spread to the States.

Today the God-given wisdom and practical usefulness of the Twelve Steps needs to be brought into the church—*not* co-opted by the church—for the church to more effectively deal with the addictions and codependencies afflicting its members and participants. There are some attempts, such as Saddleback Community Church's "Celebrate Recovery" ministry, to adapt the Twelve Steps into Christian-friendly language and usage. While there's nothing wrong with that approach, I wonder if it's necessary. All truth is God's truth, and clearly God uses the

Twelve Steps to lead folks to healing.

I think there are two reasons why the church ought to make full use of the Twelve Steps as a strategic tool in growing healthy followers of Jesus Christ. First, it's clear that Wilson's hope was that the agnostics using the Twelve Steps would come to terms with the reality of God as one of the benefits of faithfully working the steps. Christianity has marvelous insight into Wilson's Higher Power, and it is that his name is Abba and Spirit and Jesus. In fact, the Higher Power of the steps so loves lost and hopeless addicts that he became one of us so that he could bring us back from the doorstep of dissolution into the daylight of God's favor and presence.

Can someone become sober and begin growing as a person without believing in Jesus as the Son of God? Absolutely. But ultimately anyone wanting to experience all the life transformation that is available to her needs to come to terms with the personal Higher Power who is, in fact, the trinitarian God of the universe.

The second reason I believe the church should fully embrace the Twelve Steps as a highly useful tool for making healthy believers is that the church herself needs the honesty and the genuine acceptance of brokenness that is the ethos of the recovery movement. More than a few times I've actually heard churchgoers say that they "envied" recovering alcoholics because they seemed like real people who were genuine and genuinely accepting of themselves and others. Wilson exhorted his readers and fellow conspirators in rescuing others from brokenness to do whatever necessary to leave falseness behind and live in the truth. He wrote, "If you have decided you want what we have and are willing to go to any length to get it . . ." And "some of us have tried to hold on to our old ideas and the result was nil until we let go absolutely." And "half measures availed us nothing. . . . We asked His protection and care with complete abandon."[6]

Steps two and three state that the remedy for our broken, powerless and unmanageable condition is the benevolent nature and power of God, who is willing to help and heal us. It is crucial that we then turn our lives over to God for his purposes and work. Steps four through nine are the things we must do in cooperation with God to change the trajectory of our lives. We clean up what we can clean up. Steps ten through twelve are the ongoing hard work of transformation that always requires our effort. Change isn't easy; that's why so few people actually do it. But it is possible.

Though the Twelve Steps are described as a program of spiritual recovery and growth, the word *program* can be misleading. What we mean by *program* is that the steps are an arrangement of the elements of recovery for spiritual growth that hopefully we each pick up as we need them. The steps are arranged in a helpful progression of growth and discovery for life change, but they are not an exact formula—in the same way that there is no exact formula for how we come to know and develop our life with God. There are no perfect theologies or confessions of faith that adequately explain the mystery of God. Rather, we do our best at cobbling together the pieces of truth God gives us about himself, the world and ourselves. So it is with spiritual growth: we practice the elements of discarding the old life and taking up the new, but there is a need for profound humility and acceptance of divine mystery.

Behaviors Have to Change

There are things we have to stop doing; there are things we must begin to do. Paul called it "putting off" and "putting on" specific behaviors (see Colossians 3:12-17). Many of us have a romanticized view of the power and desire of God to engage us in life change. It's as if once we actually become willing (to acknowledge God, to own our culpability and to acquiesce to his program), then God will swoop in and help us. Even one of the old slogans of the Twelve Step program, "Let go and let God," is often misapplied in this way. It's almost as if we don't really have to work at it anymore.

N. T. Wright makes the observation that the theologically liberal tend to dismiss the specificity of what amounts to wrong behavior, and conservatives are so concerned that God's grace might be displaced by our efforts that we don't think we need to apply ourselves; grace will be sufficient.[7] The cosmic forces that encourage spiritual entropy deviously nullify the power of grace through these two approaches to misapplying it. The only way a human can actually change is by the power of God's grace applied on our behalf. But as he calls us, we must follow. And we have to walk to do that. Put another way, there are things we cannot achieve without God's help, and there are things in our lives he will not do without our participation.

As we "work our program" and do the personal inventory of step four, which of our behaviors have gotten us in the most trouble and have hurt the most people? This becomes our personalized list of things we should be "putting off," as Paul might say. As we live in the ongoing work of step ten, there will always be new things to change. What I'm saying is that if one of my character deficiencies is anger, it will not be enough to excuse it by saying, "God understands I have this weakness and God is gracious and I'm forgiven, so I'm not going to beat myself up anymore over my anger," and let it go at that.

God never intends to leave us where he finds us. He takes us on into deeper experiences of growth, change and becoming fully integrated. But neither can I simply pray, "My anger is a problem. Oh God, by your awesome power and good will, heal me of my anger." That's a start, but it's not enough. God will not do for us what he wants us to do for ourselves; and we cannot do what we truly need to do without God's help. He's made us so we need him and we need each other.

It turns out that anger is a problem I have. Dealing with it starts with recognizing the problem and then asking God for help. But I have things I must do to "put off" anger. Essential to the work is detecting the faulty thinking that runs underneath the observable level of my stream of consciousness. Very few of us actively think, *It's okay to be angry*, but deeper in our consciousness is exactly that thought. There may be other convictions, and there may be other issues that affect us, and often we need help in fishing them out of our stream. God has made us to need each other, so why would we think we can see ourselves accurately or figure out what is flawed in our thinking all on our own?

Having said that, we do have to apply ourselves. Paul wrote to the church at Philippi that the effects of Christ's coming would be to make of his followers a group of people who would be characterized by sharing an abundant spirit of mutual love and joyous obedience. God would work in them individually and collectively to bring this about, but they also would have to "work out [their] salvation with fear and trembling" (Philippians 2:1-13). The application of ourselves is the "putting on" of new behaviors, and it takes personal discipline and time to do it. Dallas Willard writes, "Others can help us in certain ways, but we must act. We must act wisely and consistently over a long period of time."[8]

The goal of transformation is really the formation of a new character, a new set of thinking patterns, a new sorter and handler for our thoughts and our feelings. This is the replacement of one heart with another, or the upgrading of our heart. For our heart is where our will is, and our will is the sorter of feelings and thoughts that must be changed.

What I'm talking about is self-control, the control or management of our mental and emotional and physical resources to a spiritual focus or aim. In Christian teaching, this is the practice of putting on the new self (see Ephesians 4:24; Colossians 3:10) or dropping the old ways of thinking, feeling and behaving, and taking up new ways of thinking, feeling and behaving ("putting on Christ"). It takes effort, repetition and practice until the old ways become more or less forgotten and the new ways become second nature—or primary nature. It's all to the purpose of living a life where the love of God and doing life with God is our primary aim consciously and subconsciously.

If we're really interested in living a life of integrity, of wholeness and of blessing, this changing of the patterns of our minds is nonnegotiable. This is true for everyone, addict or not. This is tough for everyone, addict or not.

But addicts have a hidden hiccup—a kink in their chemistry—that is known to God, of course, and of no surprise to him, but often escapes our attention. Our brains have an extra circuit we've developed. This can be dealt with—it has to be dealt with—but it makes the process of change harder. I don't write this to make addicts feel badly for themselves— or the reverse, for them to have a sort of inverted pride because of how tough they have it. Everybody's life is tough. Everyone has challenges. For addicts, one of the additional challenges is the extra circuitry. It *does* make change harder, but when it happens, the freedom is all the sweeter. And great, great glory is God's when an addict experiences genuine transformation.

Thinking and the Highway of Life

What do I mean by this extra circuitry that addicts have to deal with in pursuing life change? Think about highway driving, especially out of urban areas, out in the country. Often you'll see frontage roads, long ribbons of roads that run parallel to the highway. The highway doesn't have stop signs or intersections like the frontage roads do. You can go in the same direction on either one, but one has no interruptions while the other makes you go slower and provides opportunities to turn in a different direction.

Think with me for a minute about an ordinary man—not an addict—and consider how his sexual behavior might be likened to traveling down the interstate highway. He is married, perhaps, or even if not, regards his sexuality as a gift that is to be expressed in self-restrained, healthy ways. He says, "My sexuality is a gift from God; I want to do my life with God and in God. I want to use my sexuality in a healthy and integrated way." Good! But no one is perfect. We all stray.

So he heads down the Highway of Life, and there are frontage roads. From time to time he gets distracted or tempted by something he sees, and he leaves the highway. He goes off onto a frontage road. Maybe it's somewhere he didn't originally intend to go, or maybe he thinks through the distraction, overrules the temptation and at his earliest opportunity gets back on the highway. This is life: challenges, distractions, diversions and efforts to keep moving along the Highway of Life in a way of integrity and health.

Like the regular man, the man (or woman) who struggles with compulsive sexual behaviors has the same frontage roads to deal with, but he also has to deal with an unfortunate combination of factors that have developed (hang in with me here;

this may seem a bit too fantastic, but let your imagination run with me). The psychobiological patterns of compulsion I discussed in the previous chapter act on a neuronal pathway. So our traveler is flying down the Highway of Life, and all of a sudden his alternative circuitry kicks on and his thoughts/feelings/actions jump through an invisible hole—better, a trapdoor—in his highway. Suddenly he's on an entirely different, alternative, underground highway. It's not the frontage road. It's the expressway to hell. It's devoid of the light of God. It is *not* good. And this diversion happened in an instant. This is the disintegrated life, the split life of the addict.

Once on that underground highway, the addict has to take the road to its self-destructive destination or find an escape route back onto the main road and back into the light. It's an exhausting way to live; it's the way addicts live until they move into sustained recovery.

Extra kink in the brain chemistry or not, all of us have to change the ways our minds work. That is, we have to change how we utilize our stream of consciousness, alter what thoughts and feelings are in our stream and make different choices about what we do with our thoughts. This is the changing of the mind Paul refers to when he speaks of those who are intent on genuinely following Christ (living the fully redeemed life even while they are still in this world). It means learning to regard their whole life as belonging to God on a day-by-day basis. And they see living that way as a daily offering of their whole self in genuine worship of God. They change the patterns of their thinking so they can truly sort out the thoughts and feelings they have and the input from the world around them, match all of it and sort all of it according to the being-installed patterns of Christ, and therefore come to clarity—on a moment-by-moment basis—as to what God's will for them is (see Romans 12:1-2).[9]

This transformation of the mind cannot happen unless we think clearly and change the way we think. To do that, we have to rediscover and deploy the ancient discipline of meditation. Why is meditation necessary? Because simply exercising the will alone, saying to myself, *It's really wrong for me to get impatient; I'm going to be more relaxed,* doesn't work. Why not? Because I can exercise my willpower to be patient and I'll have some success. But that success is only good until there is a disruption in that train of thought. Once I'm disrupted and then stressed or surprised, I resort to my default pattern: irritability. I have set channels of thinking and reacting, so I need to create new ones. Meditation creates new channels that I can use if I want to alter my behavior.

It's an unfortunate reality that some Western Christians feel squeamish about meditation, believing it's a New Age thing or an Eastern thing. All of us interested in a genuine and integrated spirituality need to understand the origins of our faith. Christianity is an Eastern religion that has migrated to the West. More importantly, all truth is God's truth. Our thinking patterns in this world are as disordered as the world is—that's actually *why* this realm is so disordered—and the sorting and clarifying that comes through the disciplined use of meditation is not an option but a necessity for genuine life change. In truth, meditation is a Christian practice, the pathway to a changed mind and a transformed life.

Again, the addicted person has an additional set of roads or additional circuitry to deal with, but the principles of life change for the compulsive person are the same as for everyone else. We have to recognize our brokenness. We have to have God's help. We have to stop doing some old things. We have to start doing some new things. And to do that we have to change the ways our mind works. We do this by creating new thought pathways over disciplined, lengthy periods. This is what meditation is. In many cases, we need the assistance of a therapist, mentor or counselor along the way. We have to have others. This is spiritual transformation.

Transformation Is Difficult and Rarely Done

Actually, I don't think very many people experience genuine spiritual transformation, just because it is so hard. I'm not referring only to people with compulsive behaviors, but to everyone. And because it is so hard, where does a person find the motivation to do the tough work of life change?

Ron Martoia is a writer and thinker who's been very helpful to the spiritual community my wife and I have been part of for the last few years, and he's helped me to understand there are "catalysts" that cause us to pursue change.

One motivator that can move us to work at genuine life change is *pain*. The greatest motivator for my own efforts to change has been the anguish I have caused myself. A life crash, suffering or intense pain are all instrumental in effecting life change. Pain is a major motivator for all of us who truly break through the humdrum and fog of self-satisfaction to work toward a different life.

Personal transformation can also be catalyzed by *deep experiences of love* and *habituated practices over a long period*. As Ron puts it, "Deep Love, Deep Pain and Contemplative Practice, they are the big three . . . and usually it is deep pain that catalyzes. The only one we can cultivate is the third one, though. The other two are gifts given sovereignly."[10]

When life is difficult, when pain hits us hard enough, we're willing to do anything to get out of it, and that's when we are prone to shortcuts. But when shortcuts and reactive living don't work and the pain increases, we have the opportunity to cry out to our Creator, "Please help me; and please help me not waste this pain I'm in." That is the catalyst so many of us need for real spiritual growth.

It would be a wonderful thing if we could self-motivate by a desire to love God, love others and love healthy living. But it's the rare person who can cultivate such motivation on her own. In some cases, a deep and pervasive sense of the presence of God does move some of us to genuine spiritual transformation. But what works for most of us is to take the pain our struggle brings and instead of running the other way, run into it and use it to develop sustained, habituated, transforming practices to alter how we think and how we handle our feelings over a long period. That's how we change.

The reason one of the names and roles of Jesus in the New Testament is high priest is that he has gone to unfathomable lengths to earn the right to know our plight and rescue us from our doom.

The book of Hebrews is a lengthy, first-century sermon written to persecuted Jews who were becoming Christ followers. The author makes the powerful argument that the finely developed system of priests and offerings Moses handed down to the Israelites was a sign or type of how God intended to rescue his lost ones. Ultimately, Moses' system couldn't save anyone. This is not a failure of the system, for it wasn't intended to save. Human priests had their own sins and their own mortality to deal with, so they were able to instruct but not to effect life change in the people.

So, what was the purpose of Moses' system of priests and offerings? To teach more accurate ways of thinking about God, to prepare people for changing their identity from accidental occupants of this world to intentional loved ones of its Creator and to lead people to finding their ultimate fulfillment in the

Messiah. Jesus of Nazareth, the God-Man, who has the power and the desire to save humankind, is that Messiah. Being both human (so he could die and be an offering) and divine (so he offered for the service of his people the power of an indestructible life), he "holds his priesthood permanently, because he continues forever. Consequently, he is able to save to the uttermost those who draw near to God through him, since he always lives to make intercession for them" (Hebrews 7:24-25).

Even as the teaching of the historical church makes known the real nature of the Higher Power of the recovery movement, there is no room for boasting or arrogance on the part of Christians. There is no triumphalism here. The church offers this insight into the nature of God only because she has been granted it, through no achievement or worthiness of her own.

The church would benefit greatly from embracing our own brokenness with gut-wrenching honesty, accepting each other's brokenness with heart-changing charity and selling out wholly to the life-changing power of the gospel. With such a corporate heart, we could again become the useful tool of God's loving intentions toward broken humanity that we were intended to be.

The Crucial Role of Community

In an interview with Charlie Rose, the editor of *Sports Illustrated*, Terry McDonell, briefly touched on the Tiger Woods story. McDonell said he found it heartbreaking for him in that it's always disappointing when a figure looked up to by so many behaves in a rebellious or belligerent way, and it's all the more tragic when they lie about it. What I found fascinating in the exchange was that McDonell attributed a major part of Woods's vulnerability to personal disaster to a lack of genuine community. McDonell's view was that Woods's isolation was part of how he succumbed to a life of sex addiction and deception.[11]

Transformation never happens in isolation. We're made to need each other. N. T. Wright observes that when the way of Jesus instructs us toward the new behaviors we put on in the process of life change, they are behaviors or virtues of community. We are to express mutual kindness, humility, meekness and forgiveness, bearing with one another. Those are the verbs and actions of life together. Wright writes, "Since 'love' is the primary virtue, community is the primary context."[12]

Community doesn't automatically solve everything. From time to time, someone struggling with his life finds that his primary efforts in coming to terms with his brokenness, using the tools of personal transformation and doing all that in genuine community, doesn't result in the transformation he's longing for. There's a hiccup somewhere in the line. When this happens, if the person is working at his issues in genuine community, it's the community that will either signal the presence of the hiccup or find the path to the solution. Often we need professional guides—therapists, counselors, trained mentors—and these aren't as easy to find as you'd think, but they're there. The role of belonging to one another is to help each other over the spots we can't identify. This takes humility. But it also requires the willingness and the effort to know others and let them know us.

And it requires that we be part of a healthy community. This is where the church is far too often at fault.

The Unfortunate Message Broken People Get

It's with genuine sadness, regret and humility that I offer these next words. More often than not, broken people get the message in the church that they do not belong. They're welcome to participate as long as they don't show their baggage. The messages broken people get are these: change yourself so you fit in; go away and clean yourself up first; or hide yourself among us.

How many Christians today are struggling with hidden compulsive behaviors? How many marriages are afflicted by problems that the partners aren't willing to let others know about? How many kids are struggling with the dissonance between the spiritual values they hear preached at church and what they live through at home? What are they to do with that mixed message? How does that dissonance not invalidate the message at church or the integrity of their family system or both?

A huge problem in the church is that we are not honest about our brokenness, our struggles, our need for ongoing grace. If we celebrate diversity and accept it as a valid and healthy expression of the gospel, it can't come at the price of accepting things in ourselves that are counter to genuine spiritual health.

Sometimes in the church we celebrate stories of brokenness and redemption, but we want the redemption to be displayed *now*. We want the "victory" to be achieved fully. But most of us are nowhere near achieving victory. We're in process. Real-life transformation is messy and slow, requiring patience and waiting, work and continued effort. And it's hard. We're not good at hard.

In his book *Shame and Grace*, Lewis Smedes quotes Paul Tournier: "The church proclaims the grace of God. And moralism, which is the negation of it, always creeps [back] into its bosom. . . . Grace becomes conditional. Judgment appears. . . . I see every day its ravages in . . . all the Christian churches."[13] Too easily we sell our birthright for a pot of moldy stew.

So, if you're a broken person, staying in the church means keeping your brokenness hidden. This isn't at all what Jesus had in mind. That's why some churchgoing Christians wistfully wonder what it would be like to be an addict in recovery.

Transformation, Struggle and What I Learned

Out of the depths I cry to you, O LORD!
O Lord, hear my voice!
Let your ears be attentive
to the voice of my pleas for mercy!

If you, O LORD, should mark iniquities,
O Lord, who could stand?
But with you there is forgiveness,
that you may be feared.

I wait for the LORD, my soul waits,
and in his word I hope;
my soul waits for the Lord
more than watchmen for the morning,
more than watchmen for the morning.

O Israel, hope in the LORD!
For with the LORD there is steadfast love,
and with him is plentiful redemption.
And he will redeem Israel
from all his iniquities.

—PSALM 130

God is magnificent in his complexity and well beyond our ability to comprehend. In thinking of his unending complexity we get the notion that he loves diversity and stories. Or we consider how the world has unfolded with so many different expressions of humanity. We watch Jesus demonstrate kindness in meeting different personalities in different ways. This tells us that though we can discern patterns in human behavior, interaction and transformation, God accepts and embraces the wrinkles in each of our stories, the things that make us individuals.

Individuality is healthy, then. But I think most people who struggle with compulsive behaviors, and a lot of other people, too, take individuality too far. When we focus too much on how different we are from everyone else, it creates problems for us. If we become too focused on our own distinctions, we don't learn enough from the journeys of others. Focusing too much on ourselves sidetracks us by giving us false comforts along the lines of victimization ("no one understands me" and "my problem is that others don't care about me"). Overindulging our sense of individuality can lead us to have a false sense of who we are.

And finally, while all of us are unique creatures, if we focus too much on our own pain and our own story, our sense of being unique can quickly morph into a conviction that we are alone. Isolation is toxic to compulsive strugglers; indeed, isolation is detrimental to all the sons of Adam and daughters of Eve. We were made for community. There is a balance of commonality and individuality that is hard to find and harder to maintain. Confronting an imbalance is important to becoming integrated and healthy.

My own journey in dealing with my brokenness brought me over and over again to doing the hard work of finding that balance. I learned and still learn so much about myself from the journey of others. At the same time, I was and am a unique individual, and there are aspects of my journey that aren't reflected in everyone else's.

I had to learn to be alert to the excesses of seeing myself as unique. I knew I was vulnerable to it because it offered some compensation for what life either had never given me or had taken from me. I also learned I could false-comfort myself with notions of uniqueness because I had to fight so hard to overcome my demons. I know I'm not alone among compulsive strugglers in finding comfort in notions of grandiosity. So as I worked on my issues, time and again I had to face this ridiculous notion that I was special. It was important I did that. Part of healing is developing the humility that requires us to bow before the Creator of all our souls and cry, "Not my way, but your way." I'm no more special than anyone else; I'm no more special than God says I am.

Like every other traveler on the road of recovery, there was a hole in my soul, and nothing I could find to dump into it would fill it. My compulsive sexual behaviors were attempts to fill the yawning chasm in my sense of self. And, in reality, my compulsive behavior was a dissociative maneuver. Misusing and abusing my sexuality was not my subconscious strategy to fill what was lacking in me; rather it was my subconscious strategy of trying to cope with problems I had trouble seeing.

So I went to work on healing myself, on practicing the steps I was learning, yearning for and pursuing personal transformation. I worked hard at it, and I worked at it for a long time. I'm not done working at it.

Therapy and My Search for Healing

Over the sixteen years that began when I first went to a therapist and learned I was a "sex addict," I used seven tools to deal with my brokenness.

Therapy. The first was therapy. Almost all of us need specific and discerning help from others. It's the rare person who doesn't need counsel, and most of us would benefit immeasurably from working with the right therapist at key times in our lives. I worked with my first therapist for three years, and his help was invaluable. The therapist I'm working with now has guided me to a level of recovery I had despaired of reaching. Some Christians believe therapy is at best unnecessary and at worst spiritually damaging. But all good therapy delivers what intelligent, caring community is supposed to do for its members.

How could we not need therapy? We're terribly complex creatures. N. T. Wright says that he once heard a scientist explain that whether we look through a microscope at the fascinating world of things too small to see or gaze through a telescope at the mind-boggling expanse of the heavens, what remains the most fascinating expression of creative complexity is what is on this side of the lens: "the human brain, including mind, imagination, memory, will, personality, and the thousand other things which we think of as separate faculties but which all, in their different ways, interlock as functions of our complex personal identity. We should expect the world and our relation to it to be at least as complex as we are."[1]

Add to our natural complexity the fact that, as a society, we're much busier and more fragmented than we used to be. Life is more complex. We've always needed to talk, to get outside our heads, to live in the comfort and security of those around us who we trust. Few of us do that anymore. So when we're stuck, we need to go get help from others. And when we're stuck badly, we need a therapist. Good therapy is simply one of God's tools to heal his hurting children. So I've used therapy, and it's been essential to the good things that have happened in my journey.

Therapy has taught me that I have to practice regulating my emotions in healthy ways. As an adult, I'm learning a skill most kids learn growing up, and it's terribly humbling. But it's the only way to get and stay sober, to live a healthy and integrated life. Because of how I grew up, when my emotions were dis-regulated, I would go to one of four places: I became an angry, narcissistic addict; I became threatened and felt small and in need of protection; I became a jocular, people-pleasing co-median, trivializing and deflecting whatever was threatening to me; or I was genuine. For most of my life, when stress built up or I was threatened by something, I resorted to the first three. It was rare that I could move to genuineness when my emotions were jumbled. I'm humbled and grateful to say that now genuineness is my preferred emotional place.

Therapy taught me that if there was to be any personal trans-formation, I had to learn how to stay present to whatever was going on and at the same time transcend my environment. To transcend meant to pass beyond whatever threat or limitation I was experiencing. It meant to exist independent of whatever or whoever was threatening me. Yet I had to stay present, meaning I had to experience and be connected to what was happening around me in a real way.

Earlier in my life, that was a foreign concept to me. Whatever my environment was (lousy, painful, aggressive, pretending), I became my environment. Therapy has taught me to stay in the moment but transcend the threats of my environment by working on mindfulness. I must become mindful of where I am emotionally, mindful of where I am cognitively and mindful of where I am behaviorally. I am learning more and more to make my mind be the last judge. I have had to learn to transcend my environment by making my body respond to my mind.

Both of my therapists concluded early on in their relationship with me that I had been abused and traumatized as a young child. They came to this conviction because of my symptoms, not because of anything I remembered. When I began therapy, I had very few memories of my earliest years. They looked at my adult behaviors and deduced childhood trauma was part of my story. Honestly, I thought both of them were overestimating whatever pain or distress I might have gone through. I simply didn't remember anything.

But they pursued the childhood trauma idea, and they were right. I learned that for me there are four wires that came out of early childhood trauma. One wire is "acting out," which is repeating the trauma for self-soothing; whatever created the trauma is revisited to self-soothe. There is no shame or guilt sustained while acting out, so that is what is remembered: no shame and guilt while doing the behavior.

People who don't struggle with compulsive behaviors often wonder why those who do struggle continue to utilize crazy behaviors when they know bad consequences are sure to follow. It's because while they're repeating trauma behavior, they actually don't know there are any consequences; or better, while they're engaged in the acting out, they don't remember any previous consequences. It may seem bizarre to others, but every addict knows this is true.

A second wire that comes out of childhood trauma is "acting in," when the person becomes the victim all over again. If I've been abused, it may be behaving in a way that tells others it's okay to use me or kick me or abuse me for their pleasure. It's possible to cop this mindset without it being sexual. Lots of people in ministry "act in" and receive the abuse of others.

A third wire from childhood trauma is that of emotional and behavioral paralysis: no movement left or right; no acting out, so the person doesn't feel *shame*; no acting in, so she registers no *blame*. However she cannot transcend her environment while paralyzed or take any positive self-caring steps.

The fourth and final wire is to cope with the trauma through vocation. Help others get out of their own quagmires; care for them; heal them. This wire has its obvious benefits for others, but it doesn't help the person heal.

All four of these wires that come out of childhood trauma are ways to try to get control. The typical trauma survivor develops and uses only one or two of these. Remarkably, I discovered through therapy that I had developed and utilized patterns of behavior for all four of the wires. Having all four in my skill set made it all the harder to find and cultivate the *fifth* wire, one that comes with work and requires a guide as well as a group or another kind of support. It is the wire of cultivating the healthy person, the one that existed in the young, small person before all the other layers were laid on.

The Big Book of AA teaches that resentment is the number-one offender for compulsive strugglers. Therapy taught me that not taking care of ourselves triggers the *I'm hungry* and *I'm empty* and *I need to fill up* messages in our soul. Resentment forms around the idea that something should have happened that didn't, and we've got to fill up the hole that neglect has left in us.

Therapy also taught me that compulsive behavior was not my root problem. My biggest threat all along my journey—and to some extent this continues to be a threat—is not compulsive sexual behaviors but temptation to escape through self-harm. The core threat to me was self-destruction; everything was built on that, including compulsive behaviors. That's why addiction had so much power: it gave me relief from wanting to die. The pulpit did, too, both early and later, but my core problem was the depression that came from being traumatized.

I learned in therapy that my whole life had been constructed around chaos and that I needed to pull apart that template and replace it with a new template oriented around calm. A classic condition of someone with post-traumatic stress disorder, ADHD and anxiety disorder is to let procrastination build anxiety until the adrenaline kicks in and he can find the interior motivation to become productive. In this scenario, chaos promotes action and productivity. My whole life was recovering from the storm, being in the storm or preparing for the next storm.

Therapy taught me that my life has been about coping—and that meant making my life work was all about dealing with two stages of being: what was coming at me from outside and what was bubbling up inside. How could I make what I saw coming at me manageable? I was always depending on the triggers of others to let me know what I was going to do, who I was going to be. As absolutely necessary as it was to do, stripping away this layer of performing meant that for a very long time in my recovery, I felt like there wasn't anything left of me. The emptiness I experienced in my recovery work was deafening.

Therapy also taught me that the wiring I acquired over my years of dissociating and crisis coping is always going to be in my head. I suppose in some instances the Holy Spirit might cut a person an extra-big break by simply removing damaging wiring in that person's soul altogether. So far, the Spirit has not done that in me. But he has given me the breakthrough and the skill set to make sure I do not ever have to reengage my faulty wiring. There are things I can do to make sure I keep developing my healthy mindset and keep putting off the mindset of dysfunction:

- Practice mindfulness.

- Monitor my feelings and work at regulating them. Notice when the "needle" of my feelings is moving more widely— when I'm moving into emotion disregulation—and take steps to shortcut them back into appropriate rhythm.

- Keep building healthy patterns of thinking and self-nurture.
- Keep developing my spiritual core.
- Look for ways to grow in meaningful service and active self-giving love.
- Practice self-care.

There's so much more therapy has taught me. And I'm not done using therapy to help me maintain what I've recovered and keep growing.

In addition to therapy, I used six tools that helped me in my struggle to become free and healthy.

Reading and learning. I pursued authors and speakers who knew about compulsive sexual behaviors and spiritual struggles. I read books by Patrick Carnes, Mark Laaser and Craig Nakken.[2] I read the Big Book and equivalent manuals for Sexaholics Anonymous and Sexual Compulsives Anonymous.[3] I read articles and pursued learning about addiction cycles and what makes for healthy recovery. Valid information was essential to help me discover faulty thinking and confront false convictions with authentic truth. Good and healthy reading was helpful in changing patterns in my mind.

Recovery groups. I attended and participated in Twelve Step recovery groups for people struggling with compulsive sexual behaviors. This was an intimidating step to take, and honestly I don't know that I would have had the guts if Pam had not made it clear that this was essential, not only for my recovery, but for any possibility of us making it as well. I've not said a great deal about Pam's role in my recovery because I want to respect the boundaries of her privacy. But she has been and continues to be a remarkably courageous and loving partner to me. While the pain and costs I've brought to her are among my life's most difficult consequences, the unflagging faithfulness and genuine love she has consistently shown me are among my life's greatest gifts.

The night I attended my first recovery meeting I was scared simply walking into the room. At that time the group I attended met in a moldy, dingy back room that had to be entered off an alley. For that first meeting, I had to find the alley, the loading dock by the dumpster, the single light hanging out over the door. Gulping hard, I opened the door, walked through a bunch of stacked junk and opened another door. There were fifteen normal-looking people sitting in gray, metal folding chairs in a circle. No coffee awaited; we wouldn't get coffee until we moved to a different location—the AA room in the local Unity church.

Groups were a huge factor in helping me with my struggles. I told my story. I heard other people's stories. I found out over and over again that I was not alone. I was experiencing a piece of genuine community. I learned the protocols: Start with "Hi, my name's Tom, and I'm a recovering sex addict," which is met with "Hi, Tom." Don't jump in and speak directly to each other during the sharing (that's called cross-talk). Recite the Serenity Prayer at the beginning of each meeting and the Lord's Prayer at the end. And join in other ways of doing AA meetings. No last names; anonymity was protected. For nine years, attending public groups were key to me keeping my oars in the water.

In group meetings and the conversations afterward, I avoided identifying myself as a preacher. In general, most clergy are wary of revealing too much about themselves to others. But there I was, actually pursuing honest self-disclosure. My reluctance to identify my role as a pastor was because of my fear of what would happen if people in my church found out I was in a sexual-addiction recovery group.

A person might think that if more clergy who are struggling

with compulsive sexual behaviors were open about it, we'd change the way we handle it in the church. But that is naive. It doesn't take into account the chaos that would ensue in congregational conversations, and it ignores the nature of coming to terms with something as difficult as sexual-intimacy disorders in the first place.

In fact, someone recognized me at a meeting after they'd been to a wedding photographer and seen my picture in the photographer's samples. That prompted me to look hard for a confidential, public-figures group. Not finding one, I began one for clergy. I did so under my therapist's guidance, and the group is still meeting every week. Clergy are afraid to admit a lot of things that might undermine their ability to function in their jobs, and sex is the worst. We have to change the thinking in the church, but making martyrs out of the current pastors is not a good way to do it.

Sponsors. I've utilized two different sponsors over the years of my work, each one a gift to me. My current sponsor, Jim L., has walked with me the last nine years or so and has been a stable force for recovery, honesty, service and self-care in my life. He asks me questions about how I'm doing and sometimes about why I'm making the choices I'm making. I've not been a perfect sponsee, but he's never turned me away or discounted me. He's met me with grace and truth at every opportunity, and I can't imagine having gotten to where I am now without his help. The program teaches us that when we are really desirous of the help we need, the helper will appear.

Transparency. I became more and more transparent. Before I first went to a therapist, no one knew about my secret life. Within a couple of years, I was being open and honest with a whole group of people, including my spouse. Appropriate openness and transparency is essential to recovery; it's the only way to begin rebuilding trust. The program teaches us that "we are as sick as our secrets," and becoming open and honest is an intentional strategy in becoming a healthier person. Now, it's important to understand that no one does this evenly and perfectly. We make attempts at it and then make some progress, often followed by some backward movement. But over the long haul I've steadily increased the number of folks who know my story.

Transparency isn't easy, especially when the compulsive behaviors a person struggles with include sexual behaviors. Even when sex is not involved, though, it's important for people working at recovery to be very careful when choosing whom they'll become open with. Sooner or later, we all get burned when someone we thought was trustworthy disappoints and hurts us. Especially early on, it's necessary to exercise caution and restraint in sharing openly and in finding people who can handle our story with care and honor our trust with love.

Accountability. As a general rule, those of us who've been hurt badly and learned to survive in dodgy ways don't think submitting our plans of what to do next to others is a very good way of handling life. And we've come to that position honestly. Others haven't been trustworthy; life is dangerous; I'm the only one I know who has my best interests at heart. So it's counterintuitive to become accountable to others, but that's another tool of recovery I've used over the years, and it's helped keep me on a path of genuine recovery.

Service. The last tool is working with others. It's a nonnegotiable of recovery that we serve others, just as it's a nonnegotiable of the Christian life that we care for the poor, love one another and seek to be useful for the purposes for which the Almighty has designed us. Newcomers to recovery groups are not ready to become sponsors, but they can make coffee or take out the trash. And we can all offer kind listening to each other. Sometimes just being genuinely present to someone else is the most helpful and needful act of service a person can offer.

The other-focus of working with or serving others is the beginning of the recalibration of our hearts that makes full recovery possible. I don't think God ever blesses us just so we will be blessed. He blesses us so we will be a blessing to others *as* we are blessed. He's always several moves ahead of what we see and what we know.

Yet Somewhere There Was a Hitch

I made a lot of progress over the first sixteen years I worked at my recovery from compulsive sexual behaviors. I learned a lot about myself. I changed many of my behaviors. I grew as a leader, a pastor, a speaker. I became a better father and a better husband. I grew as a follower of Jesus Christ. A lot of truly good things happened in my life over those sixteen years. But I struggled with compulsive behaviors. I could not get to a place of serene, sustained sobriety. I could not disentangle myself from obsessive thoughts and compulsive behaviors.

What was the hitch? Did I just not want sobriety enough? Was I not willing to go to any lengths to get it? There was no simple answer to that question. There was something hidden deep in my psyche, a personal and unique hook that kept me cycling around and around.

We all want to think we're special, totally unique, especially those of us who are so damaged. Part of our healing is coming to terms with that notion and seeing ourselves as just like everyone else. Yet I did have a unique piece to my journey, and it kept me cycling. But I couldn't find it. My therapist began to say things like "I really don't want to see you leave ministry; you connect with people and they really connect with you. Your folks feel like you're down in the boat with them. But there's something about how ministry affects you, and you may have to leave for us to get to it."

I was willing to leave ministry—in fact, I was sure that I was a total hypocrite, that God must be so disappointed with me that it was my staying that hindered my church from growing faster than it was. *I am a compromised leader,* I thought. *God won't bless us when we hide our sins.* But a good friend told me that I was wrong about that; God "blesses" the ministries of all kinds of leaders who have hidden lives. My sins had nothing to do with the ministry I was leading.

If anything, my ministry became richer because of my brokenness. An elder of our church, a recovering alcoholic, began an AA chapter the first year we were in our own building. It started slowly, but began to grow. When we built our second phase, I pushed for the AA group to have its own room with a sink (for the needed coffee), a nearby "smoking porch" and round-the-clock access. When I left, ten years after the group had begun, it was the second-largest AA chapter in our state. God clearly wasn't linking my ministry and my struggle by holding back ministry.

Though some will argue that those in ministry are "called apart" or "set apart" and held to a higher standard, that is a flawed and unbiblical view of leadership. If you study in the Scriptures the kinds of leaders God used and understand the wildly unstable contexts in which the apostle Paul was writing many of his leadership qualification teachings, you get a balanced picture of genuine spiritual leadership. We have a centuries-old problem of clericalism in the church, and in contemporary expression it mirrors our culture's cult of celebrity and exceptionalism. It simply isn't biblical.

Further, sometimes those of us in the church are hypocritical about the sorts of behaviors that make for "moral" leadership.

We talk about leaders being "sexually pure," but Jesus gave a definition of what it means to disobey the commandment against adultery that would disqualify most pastors and church ministry leaders. Simply looking at someone with lust— desiring to possess or enjoy intimacy with someone God has not called you to be intimate with—is breaking the law, as Jesus defined it. And what about all the other moral requirements of living with God as the center of your soul? Why elevate sexual behaviors over behaviors of speech, honesty, humility, gluttony and attitudes toward those we disagree with?

As I continued to struggle with staying in ministry, I never made a decision about it on my own. I was always in a relationship of accountability with my wife and with several other people—all earnest followers of Christ—who continually counseled Pam and me to stay in ministry. Their reasoning was that I was trying to get on top of my problems, I wasn't dismissing my struggle, and when I broke through the barrier to sustained sobriety I'd be an even more effective servant for God's people. Repeatedly this was the counsel we received over the years that I was in ministry and struggling with compulsive sexual behaviors.

Some might say that my staying in ministry was the reason I couldn't become sober. But as things turned out, that definitely was not the case. In fact, if I'd left ministry earlier, there's no reason to believe I'd have experienced the breakthrough I did. I would have taken my brokenness to a deeper level of despair somewhere else and would have disappeared into the abyss of self-dissolution. That doesn't mean that we never need to leave an environment that is toxic to our struggle for recovery. But in my case, simply relocating wasn't the answer.

However, there was a growing price to my cycling. My depression was growing deeper, even with the aid of antidepressant medication. No one can continue the sort of cycling I was in forever, especially in the context of ministry. Those familiar with the stressors of ministry know that, like all caregiving professions, it has an unusually high burnout rate. Add to that the often unrealistic expectations of parishioners that their leader speak well, relate personally with all sorts of people and effectively administrate a volunteer-based organization—and you have a prescription for extreme stress. Put over all that the spiritual dimensions of speaking publicly for God and representing God to others in both large groups and one-on-one, and the dimensions of ministry demands are superhuman.

If all that weren't enough, I was loaded with self-doubt. Shame and self-loathing were my constant companions. I really believed I was to stay in ministry and work at my recovery and become sober. My effectiveness in ministry was a testimony to the truth of Henri Nouwen's words: "Whether he tries to enter into a dislocated world, relate to a convulsive generation, or speak to a dying man, [the minister's] service will not be perceived as authentic unless it comes from a heart wounded by the suffering about which he speaks."[4]

But it was becoming too much for me. I cried. I struggled. The last couple of years I was in public ministry, every Sunday morning—and some other mornings too—I spent a full hour after awaking trying to muster the energy and courage to move my leg over the side of the bed and get up. I'm not exaggerating; it took me an hour on those mornings to overcome the depression, anxiety and despair. Getting up to face the day was torturous. On Sunday mornings I often had the dry heaves in the shower so badly I would drop to the floor and beg God to let me die. I was absolutely coming apart.

Before preaching, I would ask God to have mercy on his people, asking him not to let my sins and shortcomings bring shame, dishonor or spiritual deprivation to them. We celebrated the Eucharist each week in our service, and after giving the Communion elements to the servers, I would kneel or sit behind the table and tell God how sorry I was, begging his forgiveness. And I'd plead with him that during the week to come he'd please, please help me to become the man I knew he wanted me to be. During those years my preaching became more and more real, my ministry more effective. But the dissonance between wanting to get to a different place and feeling so stuck in my recovery was becoming unbearable.

I was reaching the point of breakdown. The consensus of my support network was that I stay the course and keep working at it. But ministry requires a great deal from those who give it; recovery takes enormous effort; and my sense of despair was taking a huge toll. This stress was going to shatter me for good, beyond repair. But how would it play out?

8

In the Darkness, He Is There

You have kept count of my tossings;
put my tears in your bottle.
Are they not in your book?
Then my enemies will turn back
in the day when I call.
This I know, that God is for me.
In God, whose word I praise,
in the LORD, whose word I praise,
in God I trust; I shall not be afraid.
What can man do to me?
I must perform my vows to you, O God;
I will render thank offerings to you.
For you have delivered my soul from death,
yes, my feet from falling,
that I may walk before God
in the light of life.

—PSALM 56:8-13

If I say, "Surely the darkness shall cover me,
and the light about me be night," even the darkness is not dark to you;
the night is bright as the day,
for darkness is as light with you.

—PSALM 139:11-12

I thought I'd known darkness in my forty-year struggle with compulsive behavior, but it was really only a taste of what awaited me. If I've learned anything about God and the ways of living in his Spirit, it is that finding him isn't in avoiding struggle. It's finding him in the struggle. Or better, being found by him in the struggle. *The struggle is where God is.*

A Stunning Anamnesis in an Irish Monastery

For several years I took my study leave in Ireland, and the last few times I retreated to a marvelous Benedictine community in County Limerick, Glenstal Abbey. The last study leave I took as the senior pastor of the church I founded was in November of 2007. The night I arrived, I told Abbot Christopher that I needed someone in the community I could touch base with daily. I told him about my struggle with compulsive sexual behaviors and my need for direction about life and ministry.

With customary Benedictine hospitality and Christian charity, Abbot Christopher embraced me with the sort of kindness that honors the founder of his order and said he had a monk he thought would be just the man for me. That conversation with Abbot Christopher and the monk he sent to me, Brother Patrick, were tangible expressions of God's grace. For what happened during that retreat began the unlocking of my hidden difficulty and helped me on my path to freedom.

I didn't know it at the time, but Brother Patrick was an accomplished author, academic and lecturer, and like most Benedictines had the singing voice of an angel. Brother Patrick (a year later, he became the abbot himself, and Christopher took up a different role in the community) came to my room each evening the hour before Vespers and we talked. He was kind and understanding, thoughtful and thought provoking.

Over those ten days, I entered a lot of notes in my journal.

Among many insights he offered was this: he was adamant that my struggle with sexual compulsivity was a part of my ministry; in no way was I to leave ministry. God was using it and would continue to use it, and I must continue to seek his will and his healing while I performed his service.

As we discussed my journey and my struggles, Brother Patrick suggested that it might prove helpful for me to spend time meditating before a particular icon in Glenstal's icon chapel. Years before, a Dublin collector of Russian icons had given his collection to the monks with the stipulation they keep it together. The monks had their architect design a profoundly beautiful Byzantine icon chapel beneath the monastery church. It was to that chapel Brother Patrick directed me with instructions on how to stand and pray, and see what God might do. This was no hocus-pocus, but an ancient practice of centering prayer and making oneself available to the Spirit of God in sacred space and time.

The "Jesus Christ Blessing" icon is a seventeenth- or eighteenth-century north Russian icon. A traditional theme of Byzantine icons is to portray Christ as the ruler over all things. But Russian icons often deepen this theme by portraying Christ as the Cosmic Ruler who manifests his power through his compassion.[1] This icon pictures our Lord blessing with his right hand and in his left holding the Gospels, opened to the text of Matthew 11:28-30, written in Slavonic. In English it reads, "Come to me all you that are weary and are carrying heavy burdens, and I will give you rest. Take my yoke upon you and learn from me; for I am gentle and humble in heart and you will find rest for your souls. For my yoke is easy and my burden is light."

I was already familiar with both the icon chapel at Glenstal and this particular icon. In fact, in an earlier journey to Glenstal, I'd brought home a copy of this icon and for years have had it where I do my daily Scripture reading and prayer.

So on the seventh of November 2007, following Brother Patrick's instructions, I prayed and meditated in the icon chapel, using the "Jesus Christ Blessing" icon, practices which were familiar to me. Brother Patrick gave me this prayer: "Drive away the darkness which surrounds me; shed around me the mantle of your light. Help me to know your will, and give me the courage to do it."

It was a warm and nurturing time, one of praise, simply being present to the Presence. I asked Christ what he wanted me to do. "I want to be obedient to you," I told him. "I really need your help. I can't keep going on. Please help me."

My praying and meditating went on for some time. Brother Patrick had cautioned me not to expect anything, and I didn't. I was grateful to have the experience of being in this sacred space and being in God's presence. The Vespers service had begun in the church above the chapel, and I could hear the monks through the floor, chanting in Latin. I was increasingly enveloped in a spirit of love and devotion to Christ. It was a sublime experience.

And then something so real entered my consciousness, it was as if I were actually transported through time back to the two-bedroom, shotgun bungalow in which I'd grown up. I could see myself in that house; I was three or four. And then unfolded a scene between my mother and me that provided the historical foundation for the childhood trauma my two therapists had suspected.

In that one memory was the encapsulation of the fear, anger, distrust and dishonesty that marked my upbringing. And here's something very important: prior to and during my prayers in the chapel, I had *not* been thinking about my mother at all.

I shared the memory with Brother Patrick during our visit

the next evening. He declared it a genuine intervention of heaven, a piece given to me *specifically now* for my journey. Why now? Heaven had its reasons. My mother had died four years before. He wondered if she needed to be gone for me to be able to receive the memory, so overpowering was her subconscious hold on my soul. But the memory was given for a reason, and given then. The Spirit would direct how it was to be used and what difference it might make.

When I returned home, I shared the story with my therapist, and he said nearly the exact same thing. He felt the memory was genuine; it fit with everything else he knew about my story. Brother Patrick had cautioned me not to share the anamnesis episode with anyone for a while, and I kept his counsel. It was a gift from the Spirit, something to be used as he unfolded more in my journey. I'd love to say getting this piece was all I needed to get to total sobriety. It wasn't. This alone would not resolve my blockage to healing. It was essential, however, for it was of instrumental use for the work I would get to do after my implosion five months later.

I Implode My Life

On a warm spring day in 2008, I was cycling again—lapsing into lust and compulsive sexual behaviors, depressed beyond depressed. It is difficult to describe how empty and desperate I felt. I was living in shadows. While I loved the light and longed to live in it, I was able to be in the light only for short periods that were not consistent. While I detested the darkness, I was inexorably pulled back into it over and over, each time strengthening the grip darkness had on my soul. I could not find my way out. No matter how hard I wanted to be different, how much I wanted to be whole and clean, how badly I wanted to please God and be a good husband, I was stuck. The deep, deep

despair I was in had a chokehold on my ability to scrape together fragments of hope. I had nothing left to keep me going
down the path I was on.

I had not used Internet pornography since installing a
software monitoring program on my computer. But when you're
depressed and despondent, when you are desperately craving
the buzz of stimulation of the old wiring, you stop thinking
clearly and resort to default behaviors. I knew of a park where
men sometimes gathered in the afternoon, and one of the things
they did was swap porn. I went there, met a fellow and got a
magazine. For some time I'd been taking antidepressants, and
one of the side effects was that it made sexual arousal nearly
impossible. Addiction is a disease of the brain, and I was just
looking for a buzz in my head. But I was too depressed, so I left
my car and walked down a desolate pathway.

I sat on a log, the warm spring sunshine bathing me and the
wind coming up as a storm was approaching from the distance.
Normally I love being outside in moments like this, but not this
day. I was beyond hope. "God in heaven," I remember praying,
"I cannot believe after everything I've done and all the grace
you've shown me, I'm here in this place, just cycling and cycling and cycling. I can't stand this life anymore. I don't care
what you want from me—anything, anything—but I can't
stand this life anymore. I don't care what you do with me, but
you have to do something. Please." No answer. Engulfed in my
self-loathing and shame, I made my way back to my car.

I did not know at that time that someone had phoned the
local police, reporting men in the park engaged in sexual behavior. As I made my way back to the car, I noticed the winds
pick up as a storm was coming in. I also noticed that no one
was anywhere to be seen. I sat in the car, feeling like I was in a
stupor. A police cruiser pulled up and after being questioned

about what I was doing in the park, I was arrested and charged with a misdemeanor for lewd and lascivious behavior. I spent the next twenty-six hours in jail.

My life was over.

Now, I actually did not do what I was accused of. Though I would plead guilty to the charge six months later because that is what seemed the best thing to do for others, the fact is that of this particular charge I was innocent. But I was a sex addict who'd lived a double life all his adulthood and struggled with gut-wrenching shame and self-condemnation. I wasn't guilty and I was guilty.

I wasn't able to place my one call for hours, and when I did, it was to Pam. I will never know how cruelly painful I made that night for her. I wasn't arraigned until the next day, and then she came to bail me out. Our marriage was finally over. It was done.

And the incident would be in the papers, probably the next morning. There are those who like to notify the press whenever a public figure has been caught doing something wrong, and clergy and sex are a favorite combination. What we didn't know at the time was that after I called her, Pam called my sponsor and my good friend Joe. Joe began to pray that God would protect our kids and the church from the hurt and shame of my arrest becoming public. Over the next couple of weeks, Pam and I would get up each morning, raw with fear, shame and emotional trauma, and one of us would make the tentative trek out the driveway to bring in the morning paper. Gingerly we'd open it and survey the pages, looking for the damning headline. It never appeared.

Unplugging Two Lives

Twelve days after being arrested, I resigned as pastor of my church. I told the board, "You know I've been in counseling for years, that I struggle with depression and with anxiety. I'm engaging in self-destructive behaviors that are going to take me down and hurt the church. There's something hidden in me that I can't figure out; my therapist has one last tool he can use, but I have to leave ministry. The problem isn't ministry; it's me."

The board offered me a sabbatical. I declined. "I have to leave ministry. There's something about how it affects me, and I can't sort it out while I'm in ministry. I'm not coming back." They never asked what my self-destructive behaviors were and asked if I'd stay for three months to allow my successor time to get ready to take over the church, so I left the church and ministry three months after my crash.

When an addict experiences a shock to his system, especially one around the behaviors that have caused him so much trouble, he gets a short-term shock sobriety. Remember the monkey that became a gorilla in chapter three? The addictive personality or little monster monkey gets quiet when the shock hits. It's as if he says, "Uh oh, better lay low for a while," and goes to the far corner of the host soul and hunkers down. Shock sobriety. I gave myself a really good shock that April, and my shock sobriety lasted for months. That turned out to be one absolutely essential piece of what I needed to have happen.

Three months after being arrested, I preached my last sermon and left my church. The next month, August, I began the last tool my therapist had for me: intensive restructuring psychotherapy. It was hugely to my advantage that I'd worked with my therapist for six years by then. He knew me well, and I totally trusted him. I plunged into the work world he created for me: two long psychotherapy sessions a week, utilizing cognitive behavioral therapy and dialectical behavior therapy. He also introduced a third therapy into my treatment, eye movement desensitization and reprocessing (EMDR) therapy, which has been developed for victims suffering from post-traumatic stress disorder. He used EMDR each week and employed this regimen for the better part of the next two years.

Here is what had to happen for me to finally recover: I had to unplug two lives and in their place plug in the right therapy. When I got arrested, my shock sobriety enabled me to unplug my compulsive sexual performance life. When I resigned ministry and left my church, I unplugged my spiritual performance life. I write *performance* knowing that it is perhaps a misleading term. But there is a sense in which all of us perform our tasks in life, and it's in this sense I use the term. It's important to see, though, that by unplugging the two distinct, self-defining, life-performing pieces, I died to my life as I'd known it. Into the yawning chasm of my vacant soul, my miracle-working therapist plugged in exactly the combination of therapies I needed.

The Hidden Piece Is Found

The intensive restructuring psychotherapy my therapist took me through was exhausting. He told me he'd done this process with about 10 percent of his clients, and he had to monitor how often he did it because it was exhausting to him too. There were three phases to the process: the *excavation* of my past and my wiring phase; the *work* phase of taking what has been and formatting the new challenges of rebuilding a healthier life approach; and the *integration* phase.

As we made our way through the excavation phase—and remember, he had the advantage of knowing me for six years already—the day came when he tried to help me understand what he was now piecing together from the information that was coming forth. He drew a diagram of five vertical, somewhat circular lines within a cone, like a helix. These represented as-

pects of my life that intersected in such a way that they reinforced each other and blunted my attempts to recover. They
were PTSD; the learning disorders (OCD and ADHD); the kind
of parenting I did or didn't get; my mother's overarching need
for me to be "great"; and the addiction I developed as I grew up.

*Where these strands of my life intersected was where I felt the
overwhelmingly intense pressure not to change.* These five strands
had a tenuous balance; somehow I had found a way to make life
work—at a great cost, of course. But I still managed to survive,
and since I was still surviving, everything in my sense of self-
preservation was committed to not changing the dynamics of
these five strands.

The paradox of my system was that it was both resilient and
fragile. It was resilient in that it allowed me to survive. But it
was fragile in that the interdependency of the five strands had
to be protected. If I stopped acting out, for instance, anxiety
and shame would overwhelm me and crush my ability to continue to perform. It would upset the balance, and the whole
structure would collapse. It was resilient, too, in that it allowed
me to keep performing. I was in a very precarious state that I
could not maintain much longer. One way or another, this
could not last; it was going to come to an end. But would the
ending of this interdependency of strands result in improved
life or death? And just how was I going to be able to end it?

Now, this is key to understanding my predicament and what
would be required to unravel it. There were two independent
and absolute reasons why I would never be able to break my
cycle without stepping away from ministry, at least for a time.
One, I needed to go through a demanding psychological process
of restructuring, and no one has enough energy to do both
ministry and restructuring. It could be only one or the other.
Two, because my own personal wiring was such an enmeshment

of performance to survive, my ministry performance and my success in doing it masked the hidden prompts that drove me on. I had to stop performing to pull apart the hidden wires.

So, with all this interdependent reinforcement, how could this system be unraveled? One of three things would be necessary: (1) Pam would have to come to the very end of her ability to continue our marriage and divorce me. That didn't happen. (2) I would have to be found out, fired, and endure the resulting public shame and humiliation. That didn't happen. Or (3) I would have to crash. That's what happened when I was arrested. So even though my implosion and arrest were the clear consequences of my sin, in the wisdom of God they were exactly what I needed, and God used them for good. It was God's mercy.

In hindsight, I now know that five things had to happen for me to make progress. I had to make an unrelenting, rock-hard commitment to leave ministry. I had to make an unrelenting, rock-hard commitment to leave living in the shadows (acting out in compulsive sexual behavior). I had to engage in a long-term psychological therapy process called restructuring. I had to have the support of others. Finally, it also seems that it was necessary for my mother to be long gone for me to be able to do all this.

Knowing the veracity of my childhood trauma because of the restored memory was helpful, but it didn't answer how it was that my mother wielded such enormous psychological power over me. Why was her influence so captivating, and what was the drumbeat of self-destruction that reverberated so deeply in my soul?

As we left the excavation phase of restructuring and entered the work phase, we had a therapy session in which my therapist laid out for me what he was reassembling from the threads of my life. Without consciously knowing what she was doing, my mother had hardwired onto my subconscious psyche this message: "Tom, you and I cannot be normal. But if you, Tom, are truly great, if you 'wow' people and impress people so that they keep coming back; if you make people say 'Isn't that Tom Ryan something' and they go and tell other people how special you are; then the day will come when the world will realize that you are special because I, Mary Ryan, underappreciated and misunderstood, by my own suffering gave the world the great gift of my only son. . . . And, Tom, you can never leave."

When he finished giving me that summary scenario, I crumpled. My vision became blurred and my hearing was as if I were underwater; everything seemed to be in slow motion. It was as if heaven was saying, "Pay attention here; this is truth you need." So many pieces of my life puzzle fell into place. My life finally made sense to me. It was simply overwhelming. I cried, and for a while we were both quiet.

When my head finally came back up, my first question was the obvious one: "So everything, *everything*, I did in ministry over all these years was only to serve this false call?" My therapist's response was that, no, that was not the case. I had a false call from my mother, but heaven had given me genuine gifts and a divine calling. My problem was that every time I successfully fulfilled the real call, it reinforced the false one. Deep in my soul, a mean little voice would always say, "Good. Now do it again." Nothing would ever be enough.

It sounds fittingly dramatic to say that day was the turning point in my journey. Maybe it was. But maybe I've had lots of turning points. In some sense, every morning for every one of us is a turning point, isn't it? We have to decide each day if we'll keep working at moving forward or if we'll coast; if we'll tackle what lies before us or if we'll deviate to a softer, gentler path.

But this was a very significant day. For the first time, my life made sense to me.

My work wasn't anywhere near done. In reality, it still isn't done. It takes a long time to heal, to recover, to change a life. And it's terribly draining. It takes immense energy to change life pathways. That's one reason so few people do it. I'm still not done, and I doubt I ever will be in this life.

But I am sober. As I write this, I've had more than four years of freedom from compulsive sexual behaviors. I'm living a life I never dreamed could be mine.

9

God, Brokenness and Life in the Mindful Calm

Were the whole realm of nature mine,
That were a present far too small;
Love so amazing, so divine,
Demands my soul, my life, my all.

—"WHEN I SURVEY THE WONDROUS CROSS"

A friend of mine was the regional director for Young Life in our area, and he would sometimes joke that when it came to raising funds, "guilt is the gift that keeps on giving." If people feel guilty enough about what they're not doing (for God, for kids, for whatever they know they should be doing), it's easy to get them to write a check to appease their conscience. There's a lot of truth in that joke, and we probably fund more of the Christian enterprise by accessing the guilt people feel than we'd want to admit. Just as "guilt is the gift" that keeps a lot of charitable giving flowing, we all have attitudes and practices that can keep us locked in closets of loneliness and self-destruction.

One of the old slogans of the recovery movement is "God, help me not to waste my pain." It is the nature of God to take our experiences, pain and failures and, if we will cooperate with him, use them for good. Paul refers to God as the one "who gives life to the dead and calls into existence the things that do not exist" (Romans 4:17). He called me out of a death of sorts and certainly has brought me into a sustained sobriety that never existed before. As he's done this, I've begun to see a number of changes in my attitude and practices that have been vital in my journey.

These practices are in no way specific to me; they aren't even exclusive to people struggling with compulsive behaviors. Remember, addicts are just like everyone else, only more so. These key practices to finding the way of God in our brokenness belong to all the sons of Adam and daughters of Eve who long for the promises of Abraham, Moses and Jesus to be fulfilled in their lives. These are things we are all called to do, paths we are all called to travel.

We Let Go of Shame

My shame was a part of my self-deception. It always lied to me. I've had to learn to drop shame like an old shirt whenever it creeps up in my consciousness. This has not been easy. It takes a great deal of work, so prone to shame and self-shaming is my psyche.

Whenever I detect those inner whispers of "You're such a liar" or "What a poser! You aren't who people think you are" or "You are such a disappointment," I have to confront them immediately. I need to seize those shaming thoughts with the truth. This is the truth pictured by Jesus as the wonderfully loving father of Luke 15 who always looked through the windows for his child, who'd gone away to follow a bad idea with his selfish impulses. Whenever the child of this father begins to head back home, the father's longing eyes detect the motion, and the father makes an absolute fool of himself, scandalously picking up his robes and running through the fields to embrace the wayward child. This is God. This is grace. This is the truth: *we may do disappointing things, but we are not disappointments.*

That's what is so amazing about the grace of God: it doesn't discount our neediness or pettiness; it doesn't lower the bar of good works so everyone is acceptable to God, behaving however they please; it doesn't turn a blind eye to our brokenness. God's grace embraces our brokenness and says "I know" to our hurts, our fears and our stubbornness. The Old Testament word for *healing* is the same word used for *forgiveness.* In the spiritual life, healing and forgiveness are two sides of the same coin. This is a fundamentally holistic, spiritual and emotional trans-action. God's grace accepts us wherever we are, just as we are, but never leaves us there. It takes us somewhere else—where we cannot take ourselves.

The determining element of dealing with our shame is this: if God—who alone has the right to shame us—chooses *not* to shame us, then who are we to shame ourselves? And who are we to shame each other?

We Cultivate Serenity and We Leave Chaos Behind

Many of us who struggle with addiction and compulsive be-haviors experienced chaos as we grew up. Chaos in our up-bringing has a shaping influence so that we learn to live chaotically. Chaos was what I knew. Strangely, chaos was what I was comfortable with. When things were crazy, I knew what to do. When they were calm, well, I wasn't nearly as com-fortable. My anxiety shot up, and eventually I created chaos if it didn't come around again on its own.

Jesus was never in a hurry. I don't know when it was I first noticed this about Jesus, but it was attractive and strange to me all at the same time. You read the Gospels carefully and you never see him behaving in a frantic or anxious way. When the crowds and the popular following raised the tide of his good news campaign, we see the disciples getting anxious about crowd control or feeding folks or barring little kids from having access to—thereby taking downtime away from—the Preacher. Not Jesus. And when the tide of popularity went out and things were looking grim, again the disciples were nervous, edgy. Not Jesus. He was a master of the ability to "take life on life's terms" (one of the great old recovery slogans). Jesus was the master of calm.

And Jesus had emotion. He joined Lazarus's sisters in grieving the death of their brother. He laughed and he joked. He was angry, though only when he saw the abuse of two primary instruments of God's grace: When he saw the right use of his Father's house supplanted for material crassness, he was angry. And when he observed the religious leaders of the day interpreting the Word of God in a way that blocked the path to God's loving nature and grace for those who would take it, he was angry. He used his harshest language for those who kept others from being embraced by the mercy of God's passionate love for them. That tells us a lot about Jesus, his gospel and what the church should be known for.

Those of us serious about addressing the brokenness in our lives, then, have to learn to let go of chaos and craziness, and embrace calm and healthy routine. Letting go of chaos is actually coming off another drug. Whatever else we've been on—dopamine for those of us with compulsive sexual behaviors—we've also been addicted to the adrenaline that comes with chaos. Breaking my dependency on chaos was as essential and as demanding as breaking any other dependency I had. And, like shame, the way to this part of my healing was through praying, listening to what I was saying to myself, changing the script of my interior self-talk and learning to practice mindfulness.

We Do Life with the Spirit

A way to develop calm and healthy routines is to conscientiously live in active partnership with God. Doing life with God requires spending time, giving our attention and opening up our minds and hearts to share ourselves. And we need to develop routines and disciplines so we share with the Spirit of God what we are thinking and how we are feeling.

Jesus told his disciples that praying didn't mean finding the right formula of words or trying to impress heaven with lengthy speeches, because our Father already knows what we need and what's on our mind before we even say it (see Matthew 6:7-8). Then why do we need to say anything at all to the Spirit? Partly because forming our thoughts and expressing them is how we are presented, as we understand ourselves, to Another. It gets us out of our head, if you will, but unlike talking to just anyone else, we're talking to the One who can help us most with the life we've been called to live.

It's really a profoundly simple thing to do, yet very few people actually work at doing it. Why do we find it so hard? Because there is something lurking in our brokenness that does not want to be healed, does not want to see us change. Something in our human nature wants us to slink back from the threshold of transformation, to return to the way things always were, to continue to slide down the chute of self-destruction. That's why doing life with the Spirit is so hard; a part of our self actively resists our attempts to do so. Only when we are willing to pay the price required—our effort, our attention, our self-discipline—will we be able to grow this essential relationship.

It is not just speaking, but being spoken to, that matters in a healthy relationship. So we have to learn how to hear the Spirit. For sure, the beginning point, the baseline and the nonnegotiable, go-to resource is Scripture. In the Bible are at least four different kinds of literature and forty or more different authors of stories, poetry and ethical teaching material. All of this is inspired and woven together by a wooingly consistent voice: the Spirit calling to his creatures. These are inspired and inspiring words; in careful and thoughtful and heart-present attending to them, we will hear the Spirit speaking to us now and again.

But it's a relationship, not a formula. Some days we may not sense the Spirit saying anything at all, but that is the Friend being quiet in our presence. It's part of developing the relationship. Other days we hear him speaking to us through Scripture, and we must cultivate listening ears and open hearts to understand his voice.

Along with Bible reading, reading other writers helps me to develop my relationship with the Spirit. Writing down what I am learning about God and myself and then sharing those thoughts with others is also very important in spiritual growth. We need to grow our primary relationship in the context of others, not in isolation.

Just like other broken people, I'm prone to look for the easier way. In the things that matter, there aren't easier ways. There are no shortcuts. It takes time. It takes intention. It takes self-discipline. What do I really want? If I want to become an integrated human being, if I want to heal and become whole, I have to do the hard work of learning to develop my daily, ongoing, moment-by-moment relationship with the Spirit of God.

We Develop Mindfulness

I cannot stress enough how important the practice of mind-fulness is in overcoming brokenness. When our lives are hurt and when we are scattered, we learn to react to what is coming at us, to what we're feeling and to what others are doing. What we don't learn is how to monitor where we are and how we are. We don't learn how to take charge of ourselves in the moment, and this is one reason our lives are so fractured. We only live a moment at a time, and it's in the moment we need to learn to live. Learning to practice mindfulness is crucial for being able to continue to live free of compulsive behavior.

I wrote a graduate paper on John Wimber, founder and leader of the Vineyard church movement, when I was working on a doctoral degree at Fuller. I was struck by the balance of openness to the supernatural and real-life wisdom of living with the Spirit in the day-to-day that characterized John and his ministry. He lived out a fullness of spiritual experience and an expectancy of the supernatural involvement of God's Spirit in everyday living. He also understood the real work of life change.

A friend of mine, who took a course in signs and wonders that John taught, related a story that demonstrated this. Most of the students at Fuller were aware of the many street people who populated downtown Pasadena in those days, and they were specifically aware of one who occupied his portion of the sidewalk by spinning. Always spinning. Never stopped spinning. Acting crazy near a seminary like Fuller is sure to cause genuine concern and sincere attempts to provide care or assistance. One of the students in John's class spoke up one day and said he had asked the spinner why he was always spinning. The man said he had to keep spinning to keep the demons off.

I suppose if we approach this situation diagnostically, we ask if the origin of the man's condition is spiritual (demonic affliction) or mental/emotional illness. It may be both. But the class was about the operation of the Spirit of God through the body of Christ to demonstrate the power of God. So the student posed to John the question "Why don't we go pray for the guy and see if the Spirit will free him from his obsession?" To which John sagely remarked that they could indeed go and pray for him, and they might see him experience a moment of freedom from his torment. But, he went on to ask, which of the students was willing to stay with the man and work with him, helping him with the necessary adjustments he would need to make to learn how to do life another way?

What John understood was that the man—whatever the genesis of his broken life—had adapted to his brokenness. His thinking and feeling and life patterns were now contoured to his brokenness. Heal the brokenness, fine, but now the life needs to be restructured. And the older we are when we get the opportunity to change, the harder it is to restructure. This is why the practice of mindfulness is so important, so crucial to me. I got my big break a few years back, but the break itself is not the same as learning to live a different life.

Our brokenness, like that of the spinner in eighties downtown Pasadena, is both spiritual and psychological. And it requires the Spirit to heal both. We need spiritual healing and we need mental/emotional healing, and the latter requires repatterning our thinking and how we process our feelings. This is where mindfulness comes in.

What is mindfulness? It's cultivating the discipline of being aware of where I am and how I am now so that I can better manage my impulses and make better decisions. Jon Kabat-Zinn writes that "an operational working definition of mindfulness is: the awareness that emerges through paying attention on purpose, in the present moment, and nonjudgmentally to the unfolding of experience moment by moment."[1] This definition has three absolutely critical components: awareness, intentionality and accepting things without a critical judgment. These three elements help us to learn to become present to what is happening, and that opens the door for growth. For me, mindfulness is a critical practice that helps me experience real transformation.

Remember that spiritual transformation is about harnessing my thinking patterns for the desired outcome of changing and growing my character. It is the hard work of channeling my feelings so that I do not live my life only in response to how I feel. And it is the work of changing my behaviors so that they match my ethics, my spiritual values. Mindfulness is necessary for me to become the man I want to be, because my patterns of thinking, feeling and behaving have to be changed. I have to know what they are and see where they go to alter their course so I achieve a different outcome.

An oft-cited definition of insanity is doing the same thing over and over again and expecting different results. A lot of us—compulsives and noncompulsives alike—decide we're going to become a different person or that we're going to start something or stop something, and we never really do. Why? Because we never alter how we think and how we handle feelings. We have a moment of awareness of the desire for change, but we don't engage the requisite mode of change. We have thoughts and desires about life being different, but we keep doing the same things. It *is* an insane way to live. And if we keep it up long enough, we feel insane. But most of us don't keep it up very long; we grow weary and discouraged, and we quit. We give up on the dream of freedom because of the hard work it requires.

Mindfulness is the day-in day-out, moment-in moment-out work of using awareness for changing the patterns in our minds. To utilize this practice, I've had to read about it and think about it. I've discovered some practices to use, and I've developed some of my own. This requires a conscientious and continual commitment to monitor my thinking and feeling. It can be exhausting. It takes focus and energy. But it's the only way for me to take the freedom from compulsive behavior that I was granted and grow it into a lifestyle.

I find transitions really difficult. Years ago a staff member of my church told me that I sometimes had "trouble finding the clutch." What he meant was I could be abrupt in moving from one phase of work or conversation or duty to another. I think I was like that because I let events that had an intrinsic appeal or energy pull me along, requiring no focus or energy from me. But when effort was required, I often had trouble. I didn't have the energy or the focus. The old split life didn't leave much time for contemplation; guilt and shame fueled the compulsion to perform, so I kept moving until I dropped from exhaustion. Now, with the old fuels retired, I live with natural fuel and I regularly feel depleted. This is where mindfulness helps.

Often I'll stop when I'm feeling lethargy or confusion and do a brief inventory of what I'm thinking and feeling. What is going through my head? Am I dreading something? Am I anxious about something? I think in some ways this is what Jesus was talking about when he taught his followers to cultivate a steady awareness of the moment, rather than racing ahead by anticipating the future.[2] Early in my experience with the recovery movement, I heard the slogan "Yesterday is history; tomorrow is a mystery; today is a gift. That's why it's called the Present." That made sense to me, and practicing mindfulness has helped me live according to its wisdom. Perhaps the most well-known recovery slogan is "One day at a time," which helped as a reminder but didn't accomplish in my thinking what mindfulness is accomplishing now.

It's ironic or encouraging, or both, that this practice of mindfulness is anchored in the Christian tradition itself. In the desert and then the monastic traditions of the church are the seeds of mindful practice, one key element of which is monitoring carefully and then controlling our thoughts. Benedictine Sister Margaret Mary Funk writes, "Only when I sensed the power of my thoughts and was able to renounce them could I hear the ever so small voice of God deep inside."[3]

The desert fathers and mothers of third-century Egypt, then John Cassian and later St. Benedict plowed fertile ground for all of us who want to experience genuine spiritual—and therefore life—transformation. Is mindfulness only for the extra-zealous among us, the fortunate or dedicated few? No. "The work of every one of us is interior work, the practice of training our thoughts," Gerald May wrote.[4] Practicing mindfulness is doing that hard and fruitful interior work.

Mindfulness and Dealing with Post-Traumatic Stress Disorder

A great number of folks who suffer addiction also suffer from post-traumatic stress disorder. Research in the last five or six years has shown three areas of behavior that are affected because of PTSD, and significant treatment is needed. A combination of using eye movement and desensitization reprocessing therapy and other standard therapies, such as cognitive behavioral therapy, can be very helpful. Then if the person develops the disciplined practice of mindfulness, she can go a long way toward mitigating these harmful repercussions of childhood or adult trauma.

One struggle most of us with PTSD have is a higher than normal sensitivity to environmental and physical conditions. Our adaptability to environmental extremes is lower than normal and our sensitivity is higher than normal; anything from the temperature or sounds to a sweater itching can trigger anxiety; any and all transitions make all the sensors go off ("this may be dangerous"). When we have difficulty with transitions, it makes it difficult to settle in. These traits are very common in kids whose lives have been terrorized and/or chaotic.

Practicing mindfulness helps us become aware of the triggers of our environments and how to take care of ourselves in the moment. I used to have a difficult time preaching because I noticed everything and was often destabilized if the atmosphere was too hot or too cold. If the sound system was having glitches, the distraction was almost intolerable. I noticed everyone and all their movements. It was difficult to stay focused. Mindfulness practice has made a huge difference in my ability to focus and stay centered.

Victims of PTSD also have a higher than normal sensitivity to relationship conflict; when any conflict in relationships comes up, these adults have one of two responses: avoid at all costs or bully your way through. This truth explains so much of my life, and I wish I'd understood it over the first half of my adulthood. So much of my relationship disequilibrium resulted in me reacting with a fight or flight approach.

Victims of childhood trauma who have PTSD also have a longer than normal recovery period once they've been disregulated. They have a tendency to hang on to feelings longer than most people do, and eventually the feelings become moods. If this is not interrupted by an outside force, days can go by with them revisiting feelings over and over. It's a terrible waste of emotional energy, but it is what they do.

All three of these tendencies in survivors of childhood PTSD—high sensitivity to environmental and physical conditions, high sensitivity to relational conflict, and longer than normal recovery periods—require significant mindfulness work, cultivating techniques for developing new response pathways and rehearsing them until they become normal response patterns.

Mindfulness helps me with interior emptiness. A good deal of the time, I'm realizing, my scatteredness or lethargy is due to the fact that, in the moment, I'm having trouble harnessing any feelings and I can't motivate myself to do the work of thinking constructively. The feeling is that I am empty. All my life has been about filling that spot, avoiding that feeling, denying that reality. Sometimes I need life and the universe to show up and give me the next thing. When they're not doing it, I do it myself, using my old stimulants and shortcuts. So when truly healthy integration requires me to stop doing that, I have to face the emptiness that results. And this is hard—sometimes even terrifying. What if I don't know and won't know what to do next? What if it's not going to be okay? What if I don't get a job for a long time? What if this, what if that, what will I do . . . ?

Compulsive behavior is all about filling the holes in our souls where we've leaked out because we're broken people. But what folks often do when trying to cope with troubling, compulsive behaviors is trade one compulsion for another. My memories of AA meetings include rooms filled with smoke and coffee cups. Nicotine and caffeine. Is it possible that we were replacing one addiction with another? Were alcoholics filling up the emptiness alcohol sobriety exposed with something else?

I know recovery people who work out like virtual machines, training and punishing their bodies, achieving mega-endorphin release. Is that replacing one compulsive behavior with another? It depends on the balance in their life and on their practice of mindfulness. If they are putting something healthier than their presenting addiction in the hole in their soul but are doing it compulsively, then they're still back at square one when it comes to becoming a more integrated human being. My commitment is to become a truly healthy person, fully integrated, because that's the only way I can be useful and make the best amends for the life I used to lead.

And that means coming to terms with emptiness. The Spirit does not promise I won't feel empty. The Spirit does indicate, however, that if I'm willing to confront my emptiness when I become aware of it and if I'm willing to endure the discomforts of life and the empty spaces in my soul, then the Spirit will teach me to be okay with what I find in the moment. That is learning to be content with my circumstances.

One of the most abused verses of Scripture has to be Philippians 4:13: "I can do all things through him who strengthens me." People cite this verse to buttress their insistence that they or someone else can do anything they would like to do or they think they should do. But Paul was not saying that he could develop nuclear fission or fly across the oceans or wrestle crocodiles because God had given him superstrength. He was simply saying that because of the discipline of his thinking and the careful, daily submission of his feelings to the Spirit, he had developed the practice that allowed him to do whatever he needed to do and deal with life as it confronted him (see Philippians 4:11-13). Paul could take "life on life's terms" because God had empowered him and he had disciplined himself to live mindfully.

Practicing mindfulness is not filling our minds with stuff, crowding out what we find in our thoughts and feelings with a bunch of other things. It's sorting through the drawer of our consciousness and throwing out everything that doesn't belong to a healthy, growing person. If there's nothing left, there's nothing left. God will fill it when he's ready, if we let him.

Practicing mindfulness helps me stay centered. Staying centered is crucial to recovery, crucial to living in calm rather than returning to chaos. Mindfulness strips away the things that clutter my path, the anxieties that confound my calm and the distractions I automatically reach for to divert myself. When I can be centered, even when sensing my emptiness, I can be calm. And calm puts me where I need to be, because then I can be available to the Spirit. Gerald May wrote that people who make progress in recovery know they can relapse back to old compulsive behaviors, and when they feel like they're walking on a narrow ledge, they stay centered. How? "Somehow they have learned that they can't stay centered by fighting; they stay centered by simply not leaning over the edge."[5]

We Commit to Honest Relationships

No matter how lonely I was for the forty-plus years I was in the wilderness, I thought the only way I could make life work was by being safe, and that meant handling many things on my own. Besides making it impossible for me to deal with my compulsion, isolation also made me feel miserable. While I loved my wife and our children very much and while I cared deeply for some of the people in my life, I always felt deficient as a person. Because I was hiding this secret struggle, I saw myself as a pretender. Being dishonest compounded the fear that I was an unworthy, unlovable person, played off my deep-seated fear of being abandoned, and reinforced my conviction that I needed to hide.

Now I cannot hide. Hiding is toxic to my well-being, to my recovery, to becoming the mature, integrated person I am becoming. I need honest intimacy with others. We are wired to do life with each other. When we're healthy, we're genuinely connected to other people.

Paul uses the brilliant metaphor of the human body when describing the nature of those being collected together by the Spirit to follow the Way of Jesus in this world. God has so arranged things in the way the followers of Jesus are to relate to one another, Paul wrote, "that there may be no division in the body, but that the members may have the same care for one another. If one member suffers, all suffer together; if one member is honored, all rejoice together" (1 Corinthians 12:25-26).

Doesn't this sort of thinking seem idealistic if you're a broken person? Nice thought, great sentiment, but it's not going to work. Most folks don't want to deal with messy people. But that's not Paul's version of Christianity. God has wired us to do real life with each other. And if life is real, then it's messy.

I know that I still have a tendency to isolate and go my own way. I'm still susceptible to the old messages that I can't trust others, that others aren't dependable. Too many memories of being let down or betrayed by others present themselves far too readily when I am in dark, weak moments. But isolating is like death for me now; I want to do my life with those who are committed to being around me.

Here, then, is another way that the recovery movement is a reflection of the Christian movement. The agenda of recovery from compulsive behaviors is to help us integrate the disparate parts of ourselves, to pull our fragmented lives together in a healthy way, based on true life principles. The agenda of Christian discipleship is the elemental reordering of human lives by the grace of God's goodness and the responsive work of his children to be changed into people who bear the same character as Jesus. In neither case do any of us follow these paths perfectly. Perfection isn't the point. Steady progress is.

Doing life change, becoming a useful follower of Jesus, experiencing transformation, recovering—these are all expressions of God passionately reaching into our disaffected souls and pulling out of them the redeemed, beautiful creatures he desires us to be. And fully cooperating with God in accomplishing this metamorphosis in each of our souls absolutely requires we stay the course with each other. The benefit we can offer each other dissipates when we move from this community to that, from this friend to another, from this potentially engaging relationship to a different one.

Changing communities and leaving behind relationships that are potentially helpful makes us spiritually anemic. We don't do honest community with one another, and sometimes when we stumble into it, we run because it's hard. We either affect each other positively by connecting honestly, openly and lovingly and staying in that connection, or we affect each other negatively by living fractured lives and leaving others to their own fractured lives. For good or bad, we make a difference in each others' lives. "Believing we are separate, that I do not affect you and you do not affect me, is a delusion," writes Therese Jacobs-Stewart.[6]

We Help Others

Every person who's been pulled off the ash heap of life by God's grace and gone through the Twelve Steps learns that taking the message of recovery to others who are still suffering is part of the program.[7] This is yet one more way genuine recovery is a practical outworking of the teachings of Jesus. He commissioned his followers to go out to lost ones and take them the message of God's overwhelming love for them and practical applications of care (see Matthew 10:6-8; 28:19-20). Paul built on this understanding of doing life with God when he wrote that as our lives are reconciled to God, we become ambassadors of heaven, imploring others to turn to the loving arms of their redeeming Creator (2 Corinthians 5:16-20).

Earlier I mentioned that, years ago, I began a group for other pastors struggling with compulsive sexual behaviors. More recently I began a recovery group in the church community Pam and I are now a part of for men who have compulsive sexual struggles. I based both groups on the Twelve Steps, the clergy one focusing on recovery in the midst of ministry and the one at our church using the general format of recovery groups but contoured to reflect our Christian beliefs. I also meet with others who are neither in the clergy nor in my church. One of the outcomes of this work with others is that as I hear their stories, I see my own story in fresh ways.

Walking with others in their crises and efforts to deal with their brokenness has been a constant reminder of what God has done for me. It's very humbling to face how "childish, emotionally sensitive and grandiose"[8] we are, even after some time in recovery—humbling, but necessary. Helping others helps me see myself as I really was and gives me a realistic view of how far God has brought me. That stimulates gratitude and continued growth.

Helping others also gives me occasions of profound joy, humility and gratitude because I've been useful to someone else. Again, the Big Book is hand in hand with the gospel on this point: "Showing others who suffer how we were given help is the very thing which makes life seem so worth while to us now. Cling to the thought that, in God's hands, the dark past is the greatest possession you have—the key to life and happiness for others. With it you can avert death and misery for them."[9]

Making myself available to help others does one other thing: it reminds me that we don't need to be complete or perfect to be useful. God often uses people who are still in the throes of their pain and their battles. If God were to use only those of us who've attained a certain level of maturity and personal accomplishment, the focus of the help would be us, not God and his mercy. It's part of the genius of the gospel that God will use anyone. The story of Samson's great victory against the Philistines is an encouragement to me; if Samson could demonstrate the power and glory of God by using the jawbone of a donkey to slay his foes, then certainly God can use me (see Judges 15:14-16).[10]

People who don't have their act together yet are humble and honest about it help others want to work at putting their lives at the disposal of God. That doesn't let us off the hook of needing to become mature and deal with the gaps in our character. But if we wait until we're whole, we'll never be available to help anyone. A key to healthy, appropriate leadership is the nature of our motivation, more than the progress of our maturity.

The fact that Paul instructed Timothy that "an overseer must be above reproach" may seem to contradict this contention, but we need to think carefully about what he was saying. He was not saying that those who teach and coach Christ followers are to be more moral than everyone else. He was making the point that we can't simply transplant influential people from leadership positions in the community into leadership in the church. They have to know Christ; they have to know their way around the ways of Christ; and they have to show some evidence of beginning to reform their character to be like Christ's.

Genuinely spiritual leaders find it difficult to regard themselves as "above reproach"; when considering the standards Jesus set out for all his followers in the Sermon on the Mount (Matthew 5–7), who among us is perfect? The apostle has stated elsewhere that the community of Jesus' followers are no longer under law but grace. So this passage must be interpreted based not on law but on truth and grace. As Gregory of Nyssa (c. 335-394) wrote regarding this passage,

> Is this all that the apostle cares for, that he who is advanced to the priesthood should be irreproachable? And what is so great an advantage as that all possible qualifications should be included in one? But he knows full well that the subject is molded by the character of his superior and that the upright walk of the guide becomes that of his followers too. For what the Master is, such does he make the disciple to be.[11]

Paul is making the point, then, that those in Christian leadership need to be people who are progressing in spiritual transformation, so that they can help others experience spiritual transformation, thereby being formed as a community resembling its Lord.

There are days when I struggle with what I will do and how I will provide for myself and my family. I have many times when remorse overtakes me, and the pain and grief I feel over how much of my life I've wasted is overwhelming. Recovery isn't for cowards; it's really, really painful. But remorsefulness, while important and useful, must not take us down into self-pity and uselessness. Remembering there is a call on my life—just as there is on the life of every child of God—is essential. That means I have purpose and can be useful, and that keeps me from an inward, self-distorting focus. Helping others keeps me centered on God. The closing section of *Twelve Steps and Twelve Traditions* on step twelve puts it this way:

> True leadership, we find, depends upon able example and not upon vain displays of power or glory. Still more wonderful is the feeling that we do not have to be specially dis-

tinguished among our fellows in order to be useful and profoundly happy. Not many of us can be leaders of prominence, nor do we wish to be. Service, gladly rendered, obligations squarely met, troubles well accepted or solved with God's help, the knowledge that at home or in the world outside we are partners in a common effort, the well-understood fact that in God's sight all human beings are important, the proof that love freely given surely brings a full return, the certainty that we are no longer isolated and alone in self-constructed prisons, the surety that we need no longer be square pegs in round holes but can fit and belong in God's scheme of things—these are the permanent and legitimate satisfactions of right living for which no amount of pomp and circumstance, no heap of material possessions, could possibly be substitutes. True ambition is not what we thought it was. True ambition is the deep desire to live usefully and walk humbly under the grace of God.[12]

We Accept Hardship as a Pathway to Peace

For someone who spent a lifetime finding shortcuts to avoid pain and discomfort, embracing difficulties as a path of healing has required relentless effort. Some of the hardships of recovery come as the result of truly facing our own dishonesty and practicing rigorous honesty with ourselves and those around us. Other adversities come from the responses we get from those who are disappointed in us or disapproving of us. And life has a way of handing us painful challenges too.

Growing up in chaos and neglect, I did everything I could to establish control where there didn't seem to be any. Intuitively, if someone or something was threatening, I steered clear if I could. When I was in pain, I tried to find ways to make it stop—or I avoided feeling it in the first place. If I was going to survive, I had to find ways to block the threats or dissociate. Adult recovery means no longer dissociating, unlearning all those techniques of shortcutting. It means facing and feeling the pain and the threat of life not under my control—and trusting that I will survive.

Early on, the founders of the AA movement discovered a highly revered prayer written by Reinhold Niebuhr, one of the most influential religious leaders in twentieth-century America. The first three lines of the prayer have become memorialized in the recovery movement as the Serenity Prayer. But the entire prayer is a rich encapsulation of many of the salient aspects that are crucial to becoming a whole person.

> God, grant me serenity
> to accept the things I cannot change,
> courage to change the things I can,
> and wisdom to know the difference;
> living one day at a time,
> enjoying one moment at a time,
> accepting hardship as a pathway to peace;
> taking, as Jesus did,
> this sinful world as it is,
> not as I would have it;
> trusting that You will make all things right
> if I surrender to Your will;
> so that I may be reasonably happy in this life
> and supremely happy with You
> forever in the next. Amen.

Accepting hardship means having to accept my limitations. It means I have to deal with the world the way the world actually is, face myself the way I really am, and live daily with the hopeful expectation that respects the mystery of how God does things. The prayer Niebuhr wrote is useful to remind me that I have limitations but it is the nature of God to help me confront them. Confronting them means surrendering to the reality of the existence of roadblocks to my happiness and comfort. And recovery from my brokenness happens as I muster the courage and effort to change the hindrances in my life.

There is no verse in the Bible that says God helps those who help themselves. If there were, it would be in conflict with the overall teaching of the Bible: help begins with God, not with me. But it does teach that God will help me to do things I couldn't have done before. What's required is that I be willing and that I exert the effort.

As I've ardently pursued this life of dropping shame and cultivating serenity, of partnering with the Spirit and practicing mindfulness, of growing my commitment to being in healthy community and dealing with my difficulties as they are, my progress has not been even. But it's been noticeable. My life in my head is much different today than it was five years ago. My possibilities for usefulness to others are greater than ever before. My relationships are richer and my marriage healthier and more satisfying than ever.

Above all, my experience of the presence of God in worship and in daily life is keener, sharper, more gratifying. I've known and loved God since my adolescence, maybe before. But the depth of passion and the wonder of Presence I experience now are considerable. He is more. He requires more. And he gives more.

One day when Jesus was walking by the mysteriously healing waters of the pool of Bethesda, he saw a man who had been lying at the pool *every day for thirty-eight years*. Instead of commenting on how long the poor man had been waiting for the opportunity to be healed, Jesus asked him an insightful, penetrating question: "Do you want to be healed?" (John 5:6). We have to decide we want to get well. It's a question we have to ask ourselves every day.

10

Brokenness and Healthy Spiritual Community

So speak and so act as those who are to be judged under the law of liberty.
For judgment is without mercy to one who has shown no mercy.
Mercy triumphs over judgment.

—JAMES TO THE CHURCH (JAMES 2:12-13)

Nate Larkin grew up going to his father's church, became a
Christian, was educated in a well-known seminary and func-
tioned successfully in ministry while battling hidden compulsive sexual behaviors. Nate has been a pioneer, living a life
of brokenness that is used by Jesus to help others. In his book
Samson and the Pirate Monks, Nate describes the early days of
finding help in the Twelve Step movement. He read the Big
Book and decided to see a real AA meeting for himself.

My emotions were churning as I left the meeting. My spirit
was uplifted, but at the same time I was angry—furious—
that never, in more than forty years of church attendance,
had I experienced the safety, honesty, the genuine concern
and mutual respect that I had seen displayed by this com-

munity of recovering drunks. Even though the name of Jesus had not been spoken during the meeting, I had certainly sensed his presence there, and I had heard more echoes of his teaching during the meeting than in any sermon I could recall. These people were failures and outcasts, just the kind of losers Jesus had preferred to spend time with during his earthly ministry, but their fellowship was far removed from the Christian mainstream.[1]

I love the church. I am humbled and grateful for what she has given me. It is that love for who the church is and the strong desire for her to take up her true calling and be the church she is capable of being that causes me to wrestle, like Nate, with the unnecessary shortcomings that cripple the church from being what Jesus commissioned her to be. I want the church to realize her true calling as the ultimate Twelve Step community.

Dietrich Bonhoeffer wrote that we are not to try to make the church happen—when we do, we certainly wander far from the purposes of Christ—but rather we have the opportunity to experience the church Christ has for us. "Christian brotherhood is not an ideal which we must realize," he wrote. "It is rather a reality created by God in Christ in which we may participate."[2] So how do we participate in the reality Christ has for us?

What if the church looked like Jesus' community instead of the sort of things it looks like now? If the church became the genuine following of Jesus it is meant to be, it most certainly would lose a lot of people and have to reallocate dwindling resources. But it would be a far healthier, more authentic community and a more genuine expression of what Jesus called into being.

I've written about what transpired with me psychologically and emotionally after I left my position in ministry. I did not just leave a job, I also left my community. For both Pam and me, it was terrifically painful to leave folks we'd been with for nineteen years. In the ensuing months, we attended the church where we still are, and we are grateful for it. This experience has caused us to reflect on church as community.

Healthy Spiritual Community Begins with the Gospel

The foremost defining aspect of healthy spiritual community is God—what God has done, is doing, will do. God, described by some of the Puritans as a "happy society within himself," is ultimate community. If God is a community within himself and we're created in his image, then he defines what aspects of experiencing community are possible for us. If we allow our imaginations to run along the lines of how it would look if we related to each other the way it seems the Father, the Son and the Holy Spirit relate to each other, what would we see? We would see a community characterized by healthy intimacy, an absolute absence of jealousy or envy, a perfect and joyous celebration of the expression of each other.

The gospel tells us that God adopts us into his family. Jesus said on at least one occasion that whoever believes in him and his message and his Father, those are his family, his siblings (see Mark 3:31-35). The characteristics of how the Trinity relates to itself should become the characteristics of how those of us who belong to God through the gospel of Jesus relate to each other. At Jesus' baptism, the Father spoke from heaven, declaring Jesus "his beloved." Jesus deferred to his Father in all things with reverence and love. And Jesus pointed out that to blaspheme the Holy Spirit is the only unpardonable sin. These three expressions of God allow us to glimpse an interaction between them that is characterized by a generosity of mutual respect and a totality of mutual devotion. They are individual and indivisible. Therefore, the family Jesus constitutes as his church is made up of individuals who are eternally joined to each other.

As followers of Jesus are adopted by God the Father into his family and the Spirit of God takes up spiritual residence in the hearts of each one, they are a community sent out into the world to continue the ministry of Jesus. What does that mean? It means that healthy spiritual community does four things: teaches the truths about God and the ways of God just as Jesus taught them; lives the way Jesus lived by cultivating a continuing relationship with God the Spirit and behaving the way Jesus behaved; takes the message of the gospel to others; and daily responds to the prompting of the Holy Spirit and so demonstrates that life with God has broken into this disordered realm and is now available to everyone.

The gospel of Jesus teaches us, then, that healthy spiritual community is characterized by the teaching and ways of Jesus and by loving one another sacrificially. So, what does the spiritual community that is trying to be a healthy one do with people who struggle with brokenness?

Healthy Community Respects the Frailty of Humanity

It seems to me that a lot of people who call themselves Christians and organizations that call themselves churches forget or don't believe what the gospel teaches us about our own natures. As the Bible teaches, all humans are broken beings.

In his letter to the church at Rome, Paul painstakingly laid out his thinking about God, humanity, Jesus and community. He is clear that human nature is not able to adequately reflect the holiness of God. But God, in his passionate love for his vulnerable, broken children, created a path of grace, a giving of new life that washed away the brokenness of the old (see Romans 3:9-26). The gospel takes into account our human frailty and brokenness. It does not assume our ability to make ourselves right; it assumes we need God's forgiveness and his ongoing help. Perhaps because it's offensive to our egos, many people who say they're Christians don't live like they actually believe it.

Paul wrote to the churches of the region of Galatia because he'd received reports that they were misunderstanding the gospel he'd taught them by adapting it into a faith that avowed they could make themselves respectable in the eyes of heaven. "Did you receive the Spirit by works of the law or by hearing with faith? Are you so foolish? Having begun by the Spirit, are you now being perfected by the flesh?" (Galatians 3:2-3). And here he put his finger on the problem we have with the gospel. We appreciate the fresh start, the wiping clean of our slate that the good news of Jesus does for us. But we still want to be self-justified. We want to see ourselves as people who've taken the forgiveness of the cross and gotten our act together; people who are worth being saved. But we're not saved because we're worth it. We're saved because we're loved.

This subtle tendency to self-righteousness is the death knell for healthy spiritual community. When we begin to take comfort in our own progress, our own righteousness, we've so departed from the gospel of God's grace we cut ourselves off from it. Worse, we block others from it too. Then identifying the brokenness in others becomes the platform on which we erect our own testimony. "You follow me, and you can have what I have now. I was a broken, lonely man, and then God saved me, and look at me now." It poisons community because it draws lines between people, puts expectations on them that God does not and feeds the spirits of self-righteousness, moralizing and judgment in us.

On the other hand, authentic, healthy spiritual community

recognizes we are all broken and we all need grace—not just at the start of a spiritual quest, but all the way through. The result of genuine spiritual growth, of becoming more and more like Jesus, is becoming more and more humble and useful to the journeys of others. This isn't always exciting or glamorous, and we won't build huge crowds and megacomplexes of spiritual triumphalism touting this way of living. But it is the way of Jesus, and it's more satisfying and fulfilling than any other way to live.

The thing about embracing our ongoing need for grace is that it is so freeing. Rather than fearing brokenness—in ourselves or others—we expect it. It is not so threatening, nor do we need to put energy into denying it. If we understand that none of us has it perfectly together, it creates a greater tenderness toward ourselves and toward others. This is the foundation of a community that is truly loving, truly useful to helping people live in healthy and useful ways. And this is what Christianity actually teaches: none of us has it totally together; we need each other; we're all going to blow it from time to time. So cultivating a spiritual life based on ongoing repentance, forgiveness and humility creates space in our souls for God to work his wonders of transformation and space in our community to truly love one another.

Recognizing Our Mutual Brokenness, We Help Each Other

"Bear one another's burdens, and so fulfill the law of Christ," Paul wrote to the Galatian churches (Galatians 6:2). When we remember that none of us is perfect, that none of us is completely moral, that all of us need help and will continue to need help from time to time, then we have the foundation pieces of healthy community. Doing life together well means helping each other get where we're going. Greater is the joy, greater is the impact, greater is the community and greater is the glory for God.

Jesus pointed out our penchant toward selfishness when he spoke of a well-known practice of his day. Though the Old Testament taught people to honor their parents, an interesting practice called Corban developed. A person could deny his parents help or support by declaring his resources dedicated to God alone (see Mark 7:9-13). He continued to have use of his resources but was no longer obligated to take care of his parents. It made him appear to be righteous while covering how self-serving he was.

In the Gospels, it is the most religious, most "God-honoring" folks of Jesus' day who engaged in self-righteous exercises at the expense of others. Honestly, though, all of us have a nature that can be self-oriented while at the same time we want to appear to be selfless. When we are our most impressive, our most religious, we should be most concerned. It takes brokenness, humility, grace and continual schooling by God's Spirit in being genuine servants.

At the heart of it, bearing the burdens of others requires a spirit of generosity, of love. Having a spirit of loving generosity means dropping shaming, moralizing and judging. Judging each other is a human social cancer, a psychological comfort, our great moral failing. When we judge each other, we are least like Jesus.

"Judge not, that you be not judged. For with the judgment you pronounce you will be judged, and with the measure you use it will be measured to you." Jesus said this as part of the Sermon on the Mount, the masterful message he gave when he constituted his followers as the new people of God (Matthew 7:1-2). Paul applied his theology to the Roman Christians by instructing them to be careful not to judge one another: "Who are you to pass judgment on the servant of another? It is before his own master that he stands or falls. And he will be upheld, for the Lord is able to make him stand" (Romans 14:4). These clear directives from Jesus and Paul confront our tendency to judge others.

What is so appealing about seeing the flaws in another person? Perhaps it makes me feel better about myself. Judging is inherently about me, about my petty desire to build myself up, to make myself look better. And there is an insidious consolation I find in the failings of others. I don't like to face this—I think it's a very perverse thing—but sometimes I find a wicked comfort in the struggles others have. Somehow it makes me feel good about me, and isn't that sad? How can someone who has experienced grace not uniformly apply it to others? Ah, there is a need for ongoing grace in me.

I think that at the heart of being willing to let go of judging others is the willingness to trust that God will do in his children what he wants to do. It is up to them to open their hearts to him and to ask for help when they need it. It is not up to you or me to point out what's wrong with them and where they need to shape up. Those of us who are eager to see the church be healthier and more effective in her ministry need to focus our lives on steadily following and imitating Jesus. Healthy disciples do not judge others. Healthy spiritual communities focus on mercy and grace.

Healthy Spiritual Communities Earn Trust

Brokenness makes us feel isolated; we often struggle with things that make us think there is something especially wrong with us. We can never break that self-shaming until we also risk being honest and open with others. "We are as sick as our secrets" the recovery slogan goes. Where we can be open with others about our genuine struggles and the nature of our thoughts and actions, we make huge strides in the direction of healing and wholeness. If we are willing to take the steps necessary to break down our own walls of isolation, then we make a significant contribution not only to our own health, but also to the healthiness of the communities of which we're a part.

For people to let down their guard and let others in, there must be trust. And trust cannot be expected or demanded; it must be earned. I had many people alongside me during my years in the wilderness, and often I felt a strong desire to talk with them openly. I felt so guilty, so ashamed. I wanted to tell them who I really was; I wanted to be real. But I was carefully coached by those wiser and more experienced than me that I had to be very, very careful about being open. The church is often the least safe place to be a real person.

Larkin says that the very nature of how we act toward each other in churches kills honesty "because most churches actively discourage truthfulness."[3] In an exquisitely punishing passage he tells the story of one man he knew who was so guilt-ridden that in a search for some freedom he gambled that the church he was part of really meant what it said about promising freedom and grace with the gospel. After he unloaded his burden, instead of receiving assurances he was not alone, he was "ministered to" in a way that made it clear he had just declared himself the outcast among a group of understanding yet pejorative former sinners. In handing out Scripture passages he should consult, praying poorly disguised sermons of admonishment and assigning him an accountability partner who would function as a probation officer, they made it clear that his status as a member of the group had dropped down to that of a provisional level and that he would have to earn back their trust. Larkin concludes,

> To make matters worse, as he left the meeting that poor guy was struck by the realization that he had just volunteered to become the church's new topic of conversation. Suddenly he knew that the telephone lines were already humming with the latest "prayer request." Next Sunday, his suspicions were confirmed. The sidelong glances, the awkward silences, the careful distances kept by his former associates, their wives and others, verified that his disclosure was now common currency in the congregation.[4]

Is this one reason the church has such little cultural influence and is not a community of attraction to the general society? We don't live the gospel, we shoot our wounded, we make people hide, we unconsciously parade our hypocrisy, and then we have the temerity to decry the moral failing of the times in which we live. A church with this message does not deserve a hearing.

A friend recently shared with me a story of a local congregation where a couple of exotic dancers had been attending the Sunday service for a few weeks. How the congregational leaders knew these two visitors were strippers my friend is not sure. But they knew. The leaders instructed the pastor to discreetly invite the girls not to come back to church. "They're not a good influence on the kids" was the rationale. Seriously. I must tell you this episode makes me feel ill. This is so far from the church Jesus gave his life for, I feel ashamed. I want to find those women—though I won't—and apologize to them on behalf of all of us.

How does the church become a healthy spiritual community that earns the trust of her members and displays trustworthiness to the society in which she lives? She cultivates an attitude of tender respect for the sacredness of each person's journey. We show respect for the journeys of others when we withhold judgment, seek to understand and give others the same grace God does.

In chapter three I referred to a study cited in a seminar given by Drs. Todd Frye and Todd Bowman. These two professors have made quite a contribution in the field of helping those who struggle with sexual brokenness. In one of their seminars that I attended, they discussed the four core emotions all of us share: fear, sadness, hurt and joy. They made the point that so powerful is shame as a human feeling, it always trumps the four core emotions. To break through established patterns of dysfunctional behavior effectively, people need to recognize the core feelings being hidden and thwarted. And they always need help doing so.

This means if the church is to be a safe, trusted place of healing for broken people, it has to be a place for self-reflection, clear thinking and genuine feeling. My point is that for people to discover what is really going on in their lives, they have to unpack what they're doing and what false attachments are messing them up. This takes grace and acceptance. The church must work hard at becoming a trustworthy place of grace and acceptance. According to Frye and Bowman, "Grace must precede justice every time."[5]

Until the church once again becomes the place where people who are on the outside of society, folks who struggle with darkness in their souls and brokenness in their lives, know they are welcome, wanted and loved just for who they are, we will continue to be one of the least significant organizations in our culture, just taking up space and wasting people's time. We can't just feel bad about this or wish it was different. We have to change it.

Healthy Spiritual Communities Put Sexuality in Proper Perspective

It's a most discouraging and amazing thing: both the church and the culture abuse human sexuality and human sexual practice. The culture uses the preciousness of human sexuality in the most lucrative and demeaning ways. Its hypocrisy is ribald in that everything about sex is fair game for sales and entertainment. Then someone trips up in his own sexual practice—one that society has decided is taboo. Actually, the most inappropriate or unhealthy or even demeaning uses of sexuality are acceptable in our culture. Broken people, and especially people who've been abused and traumatized when they were young, are going to have a very difficult time charting their own sexual course. Most of that, society ignores; but cross a line, and that person becomes a pariah.

I'm not at all defending people who exploit others for their own gratification—especially children. Their actions are terribly harmful and need to be stopped. But they are still children of God—tortured children, misshapen souls—and they need love and help as much as anyone. Unfortunately, many aspects of our corrections system and even many parts of our offender "therapy" programs focus on shame and control as the primary tools. The humanity of the offender is discounted and discarded. Is this really how we want to treat people? It's important to remember that in the eyes of heaven, we are all offenders.

The church does a similar thing as the culture. By treating sexual behavior in a moralizing way—not dealing with sexuality in healthy and open ways, and vilifying certain practices—the church loses the right perspective on human sexuality. The culture emphasizes it by abusing it with inappropriate use. The church emphasizes it by silence, shunning and moralizing.

And then there is Jesus. Comfortable in the presence of women. Affirming the masculinity of men. Safe and humble and at ease in his humanity. In the Gospels, people were attracted to him, drawn to him, clamoring to be closer to him. For sure, some of them are impressed with the miracles of healing and his ability to feed large numbers of people on a shoestring budget. But many were drawn to him because here was a man who didn't need to put women down to be secure in his masculinity. Here was a religious leader whom working-class men and hard-core party animals liked to have in their company. Jesus was the perfect and full embodiment of a human being totally at home in his physical person, fully integrated physically, spiritually and psychologically. This is what he wants for each of his followers.

The desert monastics of fourth- and fifth-century Egypt instructed novices how to deal with eight primary thoughts. (They were primary because they occur in all people of every era; they cycle continuously within us; and it is from them that all other thoughts, intentions and motivations arise.) They are thoughts having to do with food, sex, things, anger, dejection, acedia, vainglory and pride. (Acedia is sloth, laziness or discouragement, and vainglory speaks of boasting of one's accomplishments and so was later folded into pride.)

"The order of these thoughts makes a difference because they move in a sequence from simple to complex," writes Margaret Mary Funk.[6] When the church did some of her best thinking about where our thoughts and temptations for fractured or sinful living are clustered, sexuality was only one of eight primal categories. And the highest level of disordered thinking is pride. We need to regain that perspective in the church today.

So that means healthy spiritual communities learn to restore human sexuality to a place of proper perspective. Being human means being a sexual person, and that is good. Our behaviors do matter, and we can help each other understand why we have some of the impulses we have and what to do with the way we've been formed sexually as we've grown up.

All these are natural and healthy issues that ought to be addressed in the spiritual community. When we do, we send the message to emerging generations that their sexuality is not something to be afraid of or ashamed of but is a powerful and wonderful gift from our Creator. When we teach each other healthy sexual practices in the right way and for the right reasons, we begin to unpack more of what Jesus wants for each of his followers. And we have something authentic, healthy and attractive to share with the society around us.

Healthy Spiritual Communities Have Appropriate Expectations of Leaders

Bill Hybels of Willow Creek Community Church used to say, "Speed of the leader, speed of the team." The truth is that leadership has a direct influence on the health of the organization. And in the church, the organization has a direct influence on the health of the leader. Jesus has instituted a community of mutuality, but the church's leadership is in trouble. It is shrouded in hiddenness and secrecy because of the unbiblical and unconscionable expectations we put on it.

All church leaders, because they are human, are broken, fallible people in need of mercy and truth like everyone else. The deeper we go in our walk with Jesus and the more we partner with the Spirit, the more conscious we become of our own frailties, hang-ups and brokenness. And the more impossible it is for us to hold ourselves up as the higher moral authority in our community. Those of us in the clergy who hold ourselves to be the truly moral leadership, the set-apart ones, are contributing to unhealthy leadership. But we are not alone.

The truth is that many folks in the church want to be able to think that their clergy are morally pure. Protestants are just like Catholics, but less honest, in subscribing to the dual citizenship of the kingdom of heaven. Catholics have for a very long time had the religious class—the called, the chosen, the holy ones. Then there's everyone else. In old Catholic thinking and practice, the ones taking religious vows are the ones who are in, spiritually speaking. I have a Catholic neighbor who hollers across the street at me every time we have a big snowstorm and we're both out shoveling our driveways. He must think I have "pull" with God because I belong to the religious class, so why don't I do something about all the snow? I point out I'm in sales, not management, but he's not consoled.

Protestants do the same thing; we've put clergy and celebrity ministry leaders into a sacred, set-apart class. One unfortunate consequence is that this takes the pressure off those who ride in "coach," because the expectations they have for themselves are lower. It's the classic divide of disciples versus garden-variety believers, and it's nonsense. Jesus doesn't have two classes of followers. The clergy are just like everyone else—same struggles, same doubts, same failings. They are simply no better, no more spiritually accomplished than anyone else. This false dichotomy of clergy and laity is harming the spiritual vitality of the whole church.

The expectations on clergy are not realistic and not biblical. This raises significant questions about our current model of trundling off young men and women to three-year graduate schools of religious study and then laying hands on them, declaring them "ordained." It's the same with free-church folks who feel the passion of service and the unction of a holy call, so hands are laid on and expectations of a holy life are in place. A better approach is to have a person thinking of ministry live it out for a few years and practice on a small-group basis, and then we'll see just what they're "called" to do.

When James wrote, "Therefore put away all filthiness and rampant wickedness and receive with meekness the implanted word, which is able to save your souls" (James 1:21), he was addressing everyone in the Jerusalem Christian community—no matter their giftedness or their roles. As inspired Scripture, this teaching is for all who are part of the community following Jesus. And what it teaches is in harmony with the rest of Scripture. The reality is that all followers of Jesus are still in the ongoing process of putting off the old life and putting on a new life with the Spirit of God. It is a process in which we encourage each other and continually draw on the aid of the Holy Spirit.

Why do we think that those who have gifts of teaching and leadership will be morally ahead of or morally superior to the rest of us? Is that realistic? Is it even possible? The reality of spiritual service is that our old nature and the evil still lurking within occasionally push back against our spiritual growth and service. Leaders may view themselves as morally superior but not if they are genuine servants of Christ. Genuine spiritual leaders in the Spirit of Christ serve from a posture of real humility—humility born of brokenness and sensitivity to human frailty.

Whether out of their insecurities or out of the perceived demands of their congregations, too many leaders hide their weaknesses behind the façade of being morally upright, morally superior spiritual leaders. This is not genuine Christian leadership. All genuine Christian leaders are humble, broken people, as dependent on the mercy of Christ and daily aid of the Spirit of God as everyone else.

I'm not blaming the church for how clergy have to deal with

such unrealistic demands. A good number of church leaders actively cultivate the notion of their moral superiority. We have to appear to be super-humble about it, but most of us love being needed, love being special and love being spiritually in charge. We don't have the cultural prestige we might have had decades or centuries ago, and a lot of us are not adequately paid. But we find payoffs where they can be found, and being in the first-class section of the spiritual plane with all the perks and expectations is part of the payoff.

For the church to be the community of Jesus' intention and to have the impact on society Jesus intends it to have, major changes have to be made. It has to be reformed to the contours of the authentic gospel of Jesus. It must be characterized as a community that understands the frailty of the human condition and respects brokenness in its members. The church has to build trust within her folds first and then within the community at large. Until respect, care, honor and tenderness characterize the way Christians treat each other and treat those outside Christianity, there will not be openness. Jesus always creates openness.

The church also needs to put human sexuality in its proper perspective: it is a gift, and sin in that area is no worse than sin in any other. And the church must alter the way she perceives her leaders: they are no more special or holy than anyone else. And they deserve mercy, grace and understanding. Just like everyone else.

Biblical Ethics and Sexual Behavior

By your endurance you will gain your lives.
—JESUS OF NAZARETH (LUKE 21:19)

*That was another mystery: it sometimes seemed to him that venial sins—
impatience, an unimportant lie, pride, a neglected opportunity—
cut you off from grace more completely than the worst sins of all.*

—GRAHAM GREENE, *THE POWER AND THE GLORY*

In the years that have followed my arrest, as I left my church and
embarked on a new life, it is quite remarkable how differently I
think and feel. I'm living a radically different life than I lived for
forty years. It's not just the difference between being a slave to
compulsion and then being free of it. It is also the freedom to
live and think without a shame track running in the background of every thought and experience. I never could imagine
what life could be like without it. When I think about that, I
can't help but smile. I feel joy and profound gratitude.

But the change in thinking, feeling and life has been much
more than freedom from compulsion. I have had to learn how
to feel all of life's feelings—without any buffer, any crutch, any

shortcut—and it's hard to learn how to do that. It's been terribly humbling to see how arrested some of my emotional development has been and to have to learn how to handle difficult feelings appropriately. Feelings are hard to handle, and I often feel like I'm a ten-year-old rather than a man in midlife. I did very well in interpersonal relationships, and I was a good pastor. But I was also using a crutch to handle transitions and stress. Now that crutch is gone; there is no buffer, and I often feel raw and fatigued.

Sometimes I feel devastated about the life I've lost—time with my wife and children, ministry I missed, living I missed. I'm free of compulsion and free of shame, and I am very grateful. But I also have deep, deep remorse for the hurt I caused others and the misuse I made of my life. It is a bitter grief to see how appalling my arrogance has been.

I think much more clearly than I ever did before. It's as if a slight fog that was always present and therefore unnoticed has dissipated from my brain. The clarity is almost jarring; forty years is a long time to be only half there. So I'm learning how to manage my thinking as well as my feelings. Meditation has been absolutely crucial to helping me sort things out, calm and center myself, and simply grow up. As I've sorted through my life, I've thought about not only where I've been and where I am now, but also what to make of it all.

How do we think about our lives and our selves when much of our living is flawed, compulsive and rebellious? And, just as important, how do we think about others and the way they live, especially when *their* lives are flawed, compulsive and rebellious? These are questions of ethics, behavior and how we treat each other.

We generally think of ethics as principles of right conduct. Another way to think about them is as a system of moral values. And what are morals? Usually morals are understood to be principles or concisely stated truths or rules of conduct. It usually doesn't take us long when thinking about morals to get right to the issue of right and wrong, good and bad. So when *moral* is used as an adjective, it is a judgment on whether a human action or character is good or bad. In thinking and speaking of ethics and morals, and especially if we want to be faithful to the spirit of the Bible, there is something very important to remember: we primarily are to use ethics and morals to address our own lives, not the lives of others.

But where do our ethics and our morals come from? Who decides and why? Is there a hierarchy of ethics? Is there some source that is above every other source? If we want to frame our thinking from a Christian perspective, the final arbiter of Christian ethics has to be Jesus. When he was asked to sort through the ethics of the law of Moses and determine the top of the ethical hierarchy, he made a fundamental declarative and shaping statement: "You shall love the Lord your God with all your heart and with all your soul and with all your mind. This is the great and first commandment. And a second is like it: You shall love your neighbor as yourself. On these two commandments depend all the Law and the Prophets" (Matthew 22:37-40). This towering statement has to control our thinking about all ethics—including sexual ethics.

Misusing Ethics

It is prudent for those in Christian circles who want to teach faithfully what the Bible has to say about sexual behavior to exercise great self-restraint. This includes all well-meaning preachers, church leaders and Christians who speak about moral values and moral purity. When they either criticize the culture for moral failing or fault specific people for sexual sin, one of the results is that they unintentionally mirror the culture by overemphasizing sexual practices, thereby losing a healthy, biblical perspective.

Our culture celebrates sexuality by misusing it, and it doesn't know what to do when sexual behaviors cross certain lines. A person looking for contentment in handling her sexuality will never find it in the patterns and opportunities featured in our mainstream culture. The culture does not know how to put human sexuality in perspective because its use of sex is devoid of ethics offered by our Creator. Our society's overemphasis on human sexuality makes it more definitive of the human experience and image than it was intended to be. The authors of *Modern Psychopathologies* write, "In contrast to messages from contemporary culture, in the biblical view sexuality is not the most important dimension of personhood."[1]

Yet—just as the culture does—moralizing preachers put sexuality in an unhealthy and unbiblical perspective. They overemphasize human sexual behavior, not by ignoring our Creator's ethics but by misappropriating them. They commit the same mistake as our culture: they overemphasize sex and therefore cause people a world of unnecessary hurt. If I just disagreed with their approach on the level of an academic discussion, I would probably remain quiet out of humility. But the preaching of the overmoralizers and the spirit in which their teaching is imposed on the church and society hurts people. It damages precious children of God. It is not right. It is not helpful. And it robs the church of her ability to function in our culture as the life-giving alternative to the ways of this world that she is meant to be.

The biggest threat facing the church in America isn't the erosion of "moral values" in our culture. It isn't rampant drug use or the growing divide between upper and lower classes or encroaching relativism or foreign terrorists. The biggest threat is the hiding and pretending of those who make up the church. We aren't honest about our failings. We aren't honest with ourselves, with each other, with God or with the world around us. We pretend to be people we aren't.

Some might think that because of my struggles, I want to emphasize grace at the expense of truth. But I don't at all ignore sin and its consequences. I'm not sweeping morals under the carpet so grace can set us free to live as we please. The people in the church who are overly concerned that compulsive sinners not be let off the hook by cheap grace need not worry. Any compulsive sinner who genuinely works through his recovery process will face the real consequences of his actions with genuine, profound and life-changing remorse. More than you can imagine.

Our behavior matters. Only God ultimately knows us and what we need and the best way for us to live. Though I don't care for the phrase because of how misused it is in the church, I believe we are all called to "moral purity." My issue isn't with "moral purity"; it is with how we get there and why. We get there by grace and doing life with God, and we do it for love. Too often moralists use fear, shame and scolding to motivate themselves and others to live an apparently moral life. But if love isn't the motivation and grace isn't the path, it isn't truly moral living.

So how do we go about thinking through the issues of sexual behavior?

The Bible and Human Sexuality

While the Old Testament has certain laws regarding human sexuality (see Leviticus 20:10-21; Deuteronomy 22:13-30), and a cursory reading of them would seemingly suggest that human sexuality is to be genitally expressed solely in the confines of covenantal marriage, a closer reading suggests that the true issue in the Old Testament is consequences, not character. The real issue seems to be the ability of males to be guaranteed a female virgin upon marriage and faithfulness afterward for the sake of bloodlines.[2] If you study Middle Eastern culture, this reading of the Old Testament law makes all the more sense. The behaviors of so many significant Old Testament figures re-inforce the idea that male virginity and chastity is not nearly as important as female virginity and chastity.

In the New Testament, the consideration of character takes the forefront. Of all the New Testament authors, Paul writes the most about this topic in passages such as 1 Thessalonians 4:3-6, Ephesians 5:3-5 and 1 Corinthians 6:9-10. The word translated as *immorality* or the earlier *fornication* in the New Testament is *porneia*, and it refers to the misuse of our sexuality outside the boundaries of marriage. The gist of these passages is that the person intent on using her sexuality according to New Testament ethics and morals will give expression of her sexuality only with her marriage partner. It's important to ask why.

Paul got closest, I think, to helping us understand what he and the others shaping the emerging community of Jesus had in mind when he wrote in 1 Corinthians 6:12-20 about the practice of visiting prostitutes. The principle he developed there applies to every human sexual connection, and it is this: sexual inter-course involves two people using their God-given sexuality for the purpose of reflecting the very nature of their Creator by es-tablishing and nurturing a lifelong union. He, like Jesus, based his thinking about human sexual interaction on Genesis 2:24: "Therefore a man shall leave his father and his mother and hold fast to his wife, and they shall become one flesh."

As it is the nature of God to love and love faithfully, when his children are being spiritually reformed into his character, they also love and love faithfully. It is God's nature to create, and he shares that creative power with us. So we have the ability to create others as we interact sexually and faithfully in a relationship of covenant. As it is not in the nature of God to abandon his children, it is not to be in our nature to abandon others. When we are being remade to reflect his character, we increasingly become faithful people who remain in intact relationships of life-giving commitment.

So it is that Jesus, in clarifying some of the misunderstandings of the Old Testament law, taught that if we engage in lusting for someone else, it is the same as committing adultery with that person in our heart (see Matthew 5:27-28). Why would he say such a thing? Because when we, in our thinking and desiring, take another being and use him for our own pleasure—even if it's only in our thinking and desiring—we are making an object out of a person created in God's image. Not only that, but when we add to our lusting masturbation, we are misusing our physical sexuality, which is intended for life-giving unity with another.

Lew Smedes writes insightfully about adultery, lust and masturbation: "It is wrong because it violates the inner reality of the act; it is wrong because people engage in a life-uniting act without life-uniting intent."[3] I would add that there is no life-respecting follow-through in relationship. When I use aspects of myself that are designed for uniting me with another strictly for self-gratification, I am misusing myself. I am cheapening myself. I am dis-integrating myself.

High standards? Yes. Almost impossible for some of us. I get that. But these are the standards that come from the heart of our Father in heaven, who is not mean, is not trying to rob us of good things or good times, but loves us and declares he has our best interests at heart. The biblical ethic calling us to reserve the expression of our sexuality for the context of marriage exists because sexual intercourse is meant for the developing of a union—a life-giving, mutually nurturing, unbreakable union—that reflects the life-giving, mutually celebrating and unbreakable union of the Trinity.

A Useful Application of Biblical Ethics

We should never assume that every married couple who seems to be moral in the sense we use the term is really engaging in the highly valued covenantal relationship the biblical ethic teaches. I suspect most married Christians are not intentional at all about following God's directions. But because no one is committing adultery or because there appears not to be any obvious immoral behavior, churches approve of such marriages and hold them up as legitimately Christian expressions that are counter to the cultural norm. But they may not be. Married people—Christian married people—can engage in unloving, disrespecting and alienating sex too. There are far too many marriages of convenience, relationships conveying people listlessly along the stream of life, hollow echoes of what God intended.

We must be careful in how we apply biblical teaching about sexuality, especially when it comes to judging others. The scathing judgment of some "Christian" voices against the sexual immorality of the culture and the sexual sins of some in the church totally misses the point of the gospel message. And it certainly puts human sexuality all out of perspective. For while misusing our sexuality is a misuse of our God-given lives (it's sin), it is only one way of many ways human beings misuse their God-given lives. I'm not saying sexual misbehavior is no big deal; I'm simply saying it is no bigger deal than any other misuse.

The crime or sin of sexual brokenness is that ultimately it dis-integrates or harms one created to be a reflection of her

Creator. But is sexual dis-integration any more offensive to heaven or harmful to the church than any other form of personal dis-integration? No, it is no better or worse. Therefore we ought to treat all dis-integrating behaviors the same: confront, love, change, heal and continue on.

In writing to the Galatians, Paul contrasted a life being reshaped and guided by God's Spirit with a life in which the ways of God are ignored: "Now the works of the flesh are evident: sexual immorality, impurity, sensuality, idolatry, sorcery, enmity, strife, jealousy, fits of anger, rivalries, dissentions, divisions, envy, drunkenness, orgies and things like these" (Galatians 5:19-21). Certainly *porneia* is the first thing he lists, but look at all the rest of the behaviors he mentions. And consider this passage he wrote to the church at Colossae:

> Put to death therefore what is earthly in you: sexual immorality, impurity, passion, evil desire, and covetousness, which is idolatry. On account of these the wrath of God is coming. In these you too once walked, when you were living in them. But now you must put them all away: anger, wrath, malice, slander, and obscene talk from your mouth. Do not lie to one another, seeing that you have put off the old self with its practices and have put on the new self, which is being renewed in knowledge after the image of its creator. Here there is not Greek and Jew, circumcised and uncircumcised, barbarian, Scythian, slave, free; but Christ is all, and in all.
>
> Put on then, as God's chosen ones, holy and beloved, compassionate hearts, kindness, humility, meekness, and patience, bearing with one another and, if one has a complaint against another, forgiving each other; as the Lord has forgiven you, so you also must forgive. And above all

these put on love, which binds everything together in perfect harmony. And let the peace of Christ rule in your hearts, to which indeed you were called in one body. And be thankful. Let the word of Christ dwell in you richly, teaching and admonishing one another in all wisdom, singing psalms and hymns and spiritual songs, with thankfulness in your hearts to God. And whatever you do, in word or deed, do everything in the name of the Lord Jesus, giving thanks to God the Father through him. (Colossians 3:5-17)

Look closely at this passage. Again, *porneia* is mentioned, but it's not isolated. What about "passion," "evil desire" and "covetousness"? These unfortunately characterize much of our "Christian" interactions in the church and among the clergy. Yet we tend to ignore them because they are too nebulous, too common, or we don't want to seem petty and judgmental. Ironically, we end up too often being petty, uneven and judgmental. But Paul pushes us all toward Christ's grace. Look at the eloquence and passion he exerts in pleading with the Colossians (and us) to be more and more like the Lord who loves us. We would do well to pay attention to this: "and above all these put on love, which binds everything together."

The wrath of God comes as a result of our idolatry—indeed, we experience tastes of that judgment in the emptiness of compulsive living. And clamoring over who is more moral advances the wrath as well. The grace of God and the gift of Christ's Spirit heal us and bind us together. It is this love and healing the church must focus on, not railing against the moral failing of ourselves and others.

Consider Mark 7:20-23, where Mark quoted Jesus as saying, "What comes out of a person is what defiles him. For from

within, out of the heart of man, come evil thoughts, sexual immorality, theft, murder, adultery, coveting, wickedness, deceit,
sensuality, envy, slander, pride, foolishness. All these evil
things come from within, and they defile a person." It's unmis-
takable that it matters to Jesus how his followers live. He's
making the distinction that it isn't the violation of Old Testament dietary laws that defile a person, but their behaviors.
But he makes clear that the defiling behaviors are what they are
because of what is *in* a person. While it matters how we live, it
matters more how we think. It matters *why* we live. The heart is
the key.

How many of our churches lead concerted efforts to root out
rivalries or dissensions among their members? How many
churches preach to themselves how to think generously and
live cooperatively with the other churches in their region? Envy
was one of the fuels for the church-growth movement in this
country. Envy stalks the hearts of most people, especially those
in competitive leadership, which includes many church leaders
and pastors.

If there is a towering sin of God's people over all others in the
Old Testament, it is idolatry—having anything in our hearts,
our affections, our devotion or our goals as important or more
important to us than God. As idolatry was the number-one
moral offense of the Old Testament Hebrews, it is certainly the
number-one moral offense of New Testament Christians. How
many churches examine themselves to root out every expression of idolatry? Having any affection or devotion that is as
important to us as God means we are idolaters, and that means
all of us are sinners in desperate need of mercy.

The Universal Need for Grace

And that is the point. We are all sinners—none more moral in the eyes of heaven than others. Paul wrote to the Romans, "All have sinned and fall short of the glory of God" (Romans 3:23). And we all continue to struggle with our frail humanity. So, John says, as we continue to try to follow Jesus, remember that we have a Lord who understands our weaknesses and not only helps us but continually forgives (see 1 John 2:1). He continually forgives because we all—every single one of us—continually need to be forgiven. And if we all need forgiveness, we all need to be forgiving. In a startling passage, Jesus says that if we're not genuinely forgiving of each other, we're not forgiven by heaven (see Matthew 6:14-15).

All sins are a crime against heaven. Sexual sin is a crime against heaven, others and ourselves. To misuse our sexuality in relation to others is to objectify them, disrespecting the image of God they represent, extending patterns of abuse and even supporting systems of sexual trafficking and slavery. To misuse our sexuality is to dis-integrate the aspects of our being, rather than to integrate them.

But is sexual dis-integration any more offensive to heaven or dangerous in the church than other personal and social dis-integrating behaviors? The key to biblically faithful and life-giving ethics is the intention and the attention of our heart. Is the Creator and Lover of our souls the primary focus of our hearts? And is love for others a primary characteristic of our lives? All other behavioral issues fall under these primary guides for the good life.

Our bigger crimes against heaven and the church have to do with how we treat each other. What is the motive in judging others, and why is it we elevate sexual behavior over all other behaviors? Some of us are drawn to clear, black-and-white measurements of what is appropriate and what is inappropriate. It's easier to measure sexual behavior than sexual thinking.

Jesus doesn't agree with that (think of him equating lust with adultery). It's easier for us to measure sexual behavior than what we say and why we say it (gossip) or what and how much we eat and why we eat it (gluttony) or whom we ignore and why we ignore them (who is my neighbor?).

The biblical ethics for human sexuality assume our failure and our failing and our need for grace. They are guidelines to the good life. They are the goal toward which we are all meant to be growing. We get this mixed up so often. The biblical ethics for our sexuality are the guidelines toward which the Spirit moves us as we cooperate with him. They are not the requirements demanded of us so that we will be acceptable to him. Until we get that straight, we do ourselves and others a world of spiritual and emotional harm.

Growing the Spirit's way and into his guidelines is hard work. Even with a profound breakthrough that allowed me to leave the wilderness of forty years, I still have to apply a great deal of strenuous effort to continue repairing my soul and rebuilding my life.

12

Broken Leaders and Spiritual Rehab

O Israel, hope in the LORD!
For with the LORD there is steadfast love,
and with him is plentiful redemption.

—PSALM 130:7

And all these principles [of Christian leadership] are based on the
one and only conviction that, since God has become man, it is man
who has the power to lead his fellow man to freedom.

—HENRI NOUWEN, *THE WOUNDED HEALER*

When Pam and I left our church and ministry, we were emotionally eviscerated. The relational trauma I had brought on us was responsible for that. As a consequence of my actions, we had to leave the church family we'd given so much to for almost twenty years. The shock and distress of leaving meant that for weeks we simply could not face attending Sunday worship anywhere, though churchgoing is an important part of our spiritual life and our life together. We were too raw. Sunday mornings were horrible.

After a while, we made a short list of churches we would visit to see where we would best fit in. At the top of our list was a church in the midtown area of our city, planted and pastored by good friends, Tim and Mimi Keel. We quietly slipped into Jacob's Well. Tim and Mimi hugged us and didn't ask any questions, and our healing began. We've never slipped out.

Jacob's Well had a Sunday-evening service in a space rented from a midtown church, Roanoke Presbyterian. A few years later, the Roanoke congregation concluded its long ministry and sold the building to Jacob's Well. The reason I tell you this is because that building plays a role in my story.

My mother and her sister attended a nearby Presbyterian church, and my parents married in the Roanoke Presbyterian building, because my mother's church was being remodeled. A few years later, I was born in a hospital just down the road. I was baptized and grew up attending my mother's church. Because both Presbyterian congregations were in decline during those years, the youth ministries of the two were combined. I remember spending a lot of time in the Roanoke building: Sunday-night youth group and lock-ins, sleeping bags on the unyielding concrete floor of the church hall, playing hide-and-seek, running up and down the dark and spooky halls late at night.

Fast-forward twenty-five years. My parents are divorced and my father is living alone, just down the street. Roanoke was where he went to church, and when he died a few years later, it's where we held his memorial service.

Another fifteen years and I find myself again in this same building, now the home of Jacob's Well.

Sometime after Pam and I landed at Jacob's Well, Tim asked me if I'd preach. I said I couldn't and then I told him my whole story. He said he was sorry for how hard my journey had been, but nothing I'd told him changed his mind about asking me to preach. He also shared with me how he'd shaped the church from its very beginning to be a community of honest transparency, of embracing brokenness as part of our spiritual journeys. A few months later I did preach for him, my first time preaching since leaving ministry.

For my first sermon after I'd blown up my life and left ministry for good (I thought), I preached standing in the very same spot my folks had exchanged wedding vows, in a building that had been part of my spiritual journey. And it was Mother's Day. You can't make up stuff like that.

Now, everyone's story is different. And over, above and intimately involved in all our stories is God, working his wonders in many ways. God does not waste things—certainly not our pain—if we are willing to partner with him in our own reclamation. And in the marvelous ways God weaves the fabric of our stories, he uses us to help and heal each other, if we are willing.

What I Had to Do

When I left my previous church, I felt I had one last opportunity to deal with whatever was buried inside of me, and I had to leave ministry to do it. At that point I was totally defeated; I was convinced my marriage was over, and I was immersed in self-loathing and shame. The church board had given me about six months of salary and benefits. But that was not nearly enough for me to do what I needed to do. I needed two years. At least.

I resigned my ordination with my denomination. I cashed in my pension fund to pay bills. The therapy I underwent was so psychologically enervating I couldn't work. Jimmy Dodd, a longtime acquaintance and the founder of PastorServe, came alongside me and was very supportive. Dear friends gave Pam and me both encouragement and support for which we will always be grateful. Though in many ways I lost so much, in reality I gained my life.

It is because we had truly remarkable friends who came around us and gave us emotional and financial support that I made it. But let's think carefully about all those who are still suffering in shame, isolation and fear. How are they supposed to deal with a crippling compulsion?

How is it we should deal with our broken servants? Is it right, is it like Jesus, and is it good for the church to let people who've given their lives to honest service at significant personal sacrifice to slip away into wounded despair? Wouldn't it be more like Jesus to kindly, firmly and gently hold onto them and assist them in healing?

As the next two years unfolded, because of God's incomprehensible and overwhelming grace, the skill and care of a brilliant therapist, and the love and support of our spiritual family, Pam and I finally experienced profound changes in me and in our marriage. As two years of the miraculous—two years of what Pam had for fifteen years been praying for and of what I'd long since lost hope for—became our reality, we decided that we needed to share our story with those who had supported us and those we'd left behind in the church we loved.

During the year following our decision to share our story, I had more than sixty personal encounters with folks, telling them why I'd left ministry and what God had done in my life since. One reason I did this was so I could make amends as best I was able. My struggle had made me less available to my church and my family. I had engaged in behaviors that put my church at risk of being shamed. I hadn't offered my people the leadership I'd wanted to, and I hadn't been the pastor they deserved. As much as I was allowed to, I expressed my remorse and asked forgiveness. The other reason I spent so much time and emotional energy reconnecting with so many people was to let them know what a tremendous thing God had done in my life so that they might grow in their own trust in him and so that God might receive the thanksgiving he deserves.

As I talked with people, I got one of three reactions. Most people listened to what I said and then responded with some version of "Oh, Tom, I'm so sorry you and Pam had to go through such a difficult battle and do it alone." Many of these were accompanied by some form of "I get it," or "I have struggles too" and "we all need grace, Tom." The other response we got was along the lines of "Well, I'm disappointed. But I am glad you told me. It must have been awfully hard, and I'm sorry you had to go through that." Both responses are the expression of true community.

My story is a hard one to hear. It isn't a story I want to tell. I did hurt and disappoint people, and they have every right to say they feel hurt. That is honest. But what was so gratifying was the expression of mutuality in both of those types of response. There was compassion and an agreement that life is a struggle and that we're all in this together. That's biblical community and that's what the church must recover if she is to be the healthy community of Jesus followers that this day and age so desperately needs.

There was, of course, another type of reaction. It ran along the lines of "You should have quit as soon as you realized you were a deceiver" or "You've sinned against God and his church" or "We don't believe you've really recovered at all; you're still a liar." These responses made me sad. Though I was disappointed, I recognized that I was the one who created the framework for hurt. I continue to be genuinely remorseful for the pain and disappointment I caused others. No one wants to find out their spiritual leader is a broken person. We have great difficulty accepting the reality of sexual issues in people, especially leaders.

I mention these responses not because I feel badly for myself, but because I'm thinking about my brothers and sisters in church service who are suffering today. The expressions I've mentioned represent attitudes we have to change in the church. I understand and accept the disappointment people have when their leaders fail. We need to recognize, though, that the tone as well as the content of these expressions of judgment is one of the reasons leaders stay hidden. There is an important line that needs to be maintained between honest disappointment and judgment if we want the church to be the genuine expression of the gospel of Jesus.

How does Jesus actually want us to deal with broken leaders? I am convinced that he likes sexually broken people; he doesn't just tolerate them. And he forgives them and helps them. He loves to hang out with sexually broken people and be with them. So this is just as true of ministry people who are sexually broken. Jesus' sisters and brothers, who are doing their best to serve, to love and to pass on his way of living to others in his name—all while they are struggling with their problems in isolation—are dear to his heart.

What Kind of Leadership Do We Want?

A very important question the church needs to ask herself is what kind of leaders she wants. If the church wants leaders who are able to help people become genuine and honest followers of Jesus, then is sexual "purity" or moral integrity a requisite for them? If you consider the biblical material we looked at in the previous chapter, who is the truly sexually pure or morally integrated person? I think the quality of leadership most necessary in the church is spiritual integrity that comes from an honest self-appraisal, a willingness to be appropriately transparent, a sincere desire to put Christ and his desires before everything else, and a gentle approach to helping others follow Christ.

It seems to me that it is the way of Christ to take people who are genuinely broken and are willing to face it and then out of their brokenness use them to do ministry that truly helps others and gives glory to God. Henri Nouwen cites the Talmudic story of the man searching for the Messiah and being told to look for him sitting among the poor at the gate, unwrapping and wrapping his wounds, ready to be found when needed. Nouwen makes the argument that those carrying on the ministry of the Messiah are wounded ministers, just like their Messiah: "It is this wound which he (the minister) is called to bind with more care and attention than others usually do. For a deep understanding of his own pain makes it possible for him to convert his weakness into strength and to offer his own experience as a source of healing to those who are often lost in the darkness of their own misunderstood sufferings."[1]

The church also must make an investment in the healthy development of her leaders. If we want real and honest leaders, we have to accept—even expect—brokenness in them. If we want healthy leaders, we have to keep them and take care of them and assist God in healing them.

The church needs to expect failure in her leaders and lovingly go to every length possible to help them deal with their own brokenness. One source indicates over 60 percent of clergy struggle with some form of compulsive sexual behavior.[2] I am now sure that is true. Many people enter ministry with some personal issues. Ministry itself is a high-burnout profession. Life in the church can be terribly isolating. Finding relief in sexual distractions is a drug that doesn't color one's breath or dilate one's eyes. The Internet is a perfect delivery vehicle. We shouldn't be surprised that clergy struggle with sexual issues.

When leaders are forced to hide their issues, they sweat

things out alone—where they are highly vulnerable to loneliness, self-doubt, avoidance and addiction. Right now there are
thousands and thousands of really good people serving
churches, people who care about God and want to be useful to
his purposes for his people, but they are isolated, afraid,
ashamed and scared to death that if their church board found
out about their problems they would be fired. Their fear is jus-
tified by the number of discarded leaders who had the mis-
fortune of being discovered to be just as human as everyone
else on their board and in their church.

The church is best led by truly broken people who experience the grace of God in healing and are following Jesus into
new life. That is messy, but genuine spiritual growth is messy;
true transformation is messy; trusting God and living the way
of Jesus is messy. Henri Nouwen put it this way:

> The great illusion of leadership is to think that man can
> be led out of the desert by someone who has never been
> there. Our lives are filled with examples which tell us that
> leadership asks for understanding and that understanding
> requires sharing. So long as we define leadership in terms
> of preventing or establishing precedents, or in terms of
> being responsible for some kind of abstract "general good,"
> we have forgotten that no God can save us except a suf-
> fering God, and that no man can lead his people except
> the man who is crushed by its sins.[3]

What are the benefits to the church if she recalibrates her
approach to leadership and accepts and willingly embraces
broken leaders? Her leaders will be genuinely grateful and
humble people. Her leaders will be open and honest. Her leaders
will be far more capable of entering into the lives of others and
bringing the light and healing of Christ. And her leaders will

experience their own spiritual transformation and therefore be able to show and lead the way to genuine transformation for the church. What a healthy and wonderful change that will be from the malevolent and unhealthy situations we have now!

Seven Things We Must Do

Examine our own sexual behaviors. Pastors, ministry leaders and those in church leadership need to do their own thorough personal inventory examining their lives for problems with compulsive sexual behaviors. No matter how fear-inducing this will be, they need to take personal responsibility to do whatever is necessary to address the problems they have and do the hard work of becoming healthier people. The elements of this process are awareness, honesty, surrender, commitment, retraining and rebuilding thought patterns, developing healthy patterns of behavior, and addressing all idiosyncratic needs specific to the leader and his family. This will be challenging and hard, and he will need help.

Change how we treat leaders. We need those who lead ministry leaders to radically recalibrate their approach to the issue of sexual brokenness in those who are in ministry leadership. Their commitment must be to help heal the ones in their ministry stewardship who are hurting and do everything necessary to take care of and provide for any dependents their ministers have. Denominational leaders who offer anything less must recognize they are no longer leading in the Spirit and way of Jesus and therefore have co-opted leadership in Christ's name for one of institutional self-preservation.

A clergy friend shared with me an example of what *not* to do. His denominational office sent an official message to every ordained person regarding Internet pornography use by clergy members. The message reminded the pastors that any sexual deviance—including use of Internet porn—was a violation of their ordination vows. They were offered a short-term window of opportunity to come forward and admit their problem. The implication was that they wouldn't be defrocked, but it was unclear if they'd be removed from their position. There was no mention of any help. Everyone using Internet porn and not coming forward during this opportunity was warned that they would eventually be found out and the discipline would be severe.

Now, what do you think was the impact of that message for those struggling with compulsive sexual behaviors? It was a message that guaranteed anxiety, shame and fear for everyone struggling with compulsive sexual behaviors and made them even more determined to repress their struggles and hide. And what is the result for the spiritual and emotional health of the congregations of that denomination? More fear, more shame, more hiding. How is the gospel of Jesus served by such an approach? How much better it would have been to acknowledge the significant problem hampering the spiritual wellness of their clergy and offer strategic help to everyone willing to address their issues—then remind them this will help them fulfill their ordination vows.

Some denominational leadership is fearful of scandals or struggling with insurance issues, and these are valid issues. But they will not be well resolved by using fear, control or shame. It is better for organizational leaders to develop a genuinely pastoral, rehabilitative approach to those struggling with personal issues—whatever they are—and then enlist the participation of everyone in dealing with correlative issues.

Allocate resources. We need denominational leaders to reallocate resources for conscientious and specific care and for the restoration of the psychological health of ministry leaders. This is Christ-centered stewardship of leaders and ultimately the best way to extend care to the whole church, not just the clergy. And it will make the church healthier. Healthy churches expect brokenness among their leaders, accept leaders as they are with a spirit of grace and mercy, and provide everything necessary for healing, with the goal of uninterrupted service.[4] Sometimes service will need to be interrupted, but that interruption should be for therapeutic reasons and not assumed. When ministry leaders break the law, the resulting criminal penalties are part of their amends. It's important that the church not abandon its criminal offenders, but walk with them through these times, remembering that in the eyes of heaven we are *all* criminal offenders.

Change our way of thinking and teaching in the church about human sexuality. We must become open in addressing the issues of sexual behaviors. This begins with a lot of remedial teaching on what grace really is and how spiritual community truly works. Building on those two concepts, then, we need to give people a healthy and useful understanding of God's design for human sexuality, healthy sexual expression and how to deal with sexual issues. The instruction must be in a spirit of openness, honesty and graciousness. The nature of the instruction has to be one of invitation and loving coaching to a healthier, holier way to live. We must teach our people how to think about and deal with sexual brokenness as a part of the quest for spiritual wholeness.

Include everyone in the solution. This is not a challenge for only clergy or denominational leaders to solve. This is a problem all of us need to deal with. As we help folks learn to handle sexual brokenness in their own lives and in the lives of those around them, we also need to embrace the biblical concept of the priesthood of all believers. Church folks need to be empowered by congregational leaders to acquire the necessary attitudes and skills to help heal their broken leaders as well as their struggling fellows.

Sexual brokenness, especially in the age of the Internet, appears to be an overwhelming issue, and the tendency of some leaders is to react in fear and avoidance. But if they use the gifts Jesus has always given the church—grace, truth, community, the patterns of healthy living—and trust what the Spirit of God will do in and with his people, we can recalibrate the church.

Make help available. We need to make competent, safe and effective help—including competent counseling—available for everyone who is struggling with compulsive sexual behaviors or any other area of sexual brokenness. Is this asking too much? I think not, because the vitality of the church herself is at stake. Half the people—more or less, and probably more—who will attend church this Sunday are dealing with unhealthy attachments and compulsive sexual behaviors, the effect of which is numbing them and dumbing them down. They are simply not able to be all there. Their souls are attached to spiritual obstacles and their hearts are conflicted. Their conscious ability to focus on the preaching, give full-hearted praise to God and take their next steps in rearranging their lives to better follow Jesus are compromised because of attachments and compulsion. For their sakes and for the sake of the vitality of the church, they need our best efforts at loving intervention and competent assistance.

Enhance ministry preparation. We need to change how we prepare people entering the ministry. We need to help them make a genuine self-assessment and give them all the necessary help as a standard part of the curriculum of ministry preparation. The assessment is not to weed people out of ministry service, but rather to help candidates identify and come to terms with their issues for two reasons: they will be spared troubling complications as their ministry work unfolds, and they will be far more competent in leading spiritual communities. They need to receive proficient and complete instruction in all the issues and treatments surrounding sexual brokenness, because this is a major component of what they must be able to deal with in helping people spiritually.

As we do these things, we will begin to reform the community of Jesus into a people marked by the good news she was intended to be. We will recover spiritual health and vitality in our spiritual community. And we will demonstrate a practical, life-giving and loving gospel to the world around us. The generosity of our life together and the health of our message will be buttressed by these truths:

- There is a profound and God-given link between our spirituality and our sexuality, and compulsive behaviors are always symptoms of deeper spiritual issues.

- Sexual sin is no greater than any other sin.

- We must deal with the challenges to healthy sexuality, because compulsive sexual behavior is putting a stranglehold on a vibrant, healthy spirituality in Christians and is robbing the church of her health and vitality.

- Isolation, shame and hiding are toxic to genuine recovery and to spiritual vitality, so the church has to become open, honest and accepting.

- We must bring to bear all the tools God has given us, the grace of Christ's gospel and the truth of Christ's gospel, doing honest life with each other, cultivating life with the Holy Spirit as the guide and the center of our beings, and developing healthy patterns of living—and this includes all the tools of recovery.

- There are some things we cannot do without God; there are some things God will not do without us.

- Genuine recovery—just like the genuine spiritual life—has to be founded on and fueled by love of God and ourselves; if it is fueled by shame or fear, it is not genuine recovery but another form of bondage.

Failure, Forgiveness and Reclaiming Each Other for God

What would it look like for the church to rescue and refuse to let go of broken people, but instead to love and accept them as they are and keep inviting them onto the hard path to wholeness? What would it look like for the church to anticipate that all her leaders are going to have significant, troubling struggles—of one type or another—and that they will need understanding and help? It would mean that instead of throwing people away or sending them away, we take extravagant measures to help them heal. It would mean we recalibrate what we expect to receive from leaders. It would mean we spend money and time to help them become well.

Can the church afford such extravagance? If we are realistic, the question is, can she afford any longer to keep doing what she's doing? Think of all the gifted and called leaders who are not available for service anymore because of crippling personal issues for which they never got help. It is costing the church far too much *not* to be extravagant in love, grace and tangible help.

Recovery from compulsive sexual behaviors has to be mainstreamed in the church, not relegated to the hidden regions as if the message is "go away and fix yourself; then maybe you can come back." Genuine, holistic Christian community recognizes that in some sense all of us are sexually broken and in some ways all of us contribute to sexual brokenness in our society. It takes all of us to address this reality and change it.

In the final scene of the movie *Shame*, Steve McQueen's masterful and punishing portrayal of the emptiness of sexual addiction, Brandon is sitting in a New York City subway car; behind him is a poster inviting people to a church.

If Brandon was willing to seek—to seek direction for his relationally broken life, solace for his sexual brokenness, or help discovering if there is a God who cares about him and will help him with his life—what experience would he find by risking a visit to that church?

Maybe he would find a church which is clear and definitive about what God has offered us in the gospel and the ways to live the good life. But over time would he discover, underneath that gospel message and the exhortations to follow Jesus, fixed judgments and stringent rules? Would he meet Jesus there?

Or perhaps he would find a church which is warm and accepting, embracing him just as he is and affirming that he's already on the path to God. And yet over time, while he might appreciate the affirmation and acceptance, would he also find that the messages of inclusion and affirmation only distracted him temporarily from his emptiness? Would he still be restless in his brokenness and his wandering? Would he meet Jesus there?

Might he find a church living on the two pillars of truth and grace? Would he, over time, discover that he is indeed quite remarkably loved by God and by God's people? And would he also discover that even as he is genuinely accepted for who he is, there is more to life—much more—and the way to that life is the way of love, of relationship, of relinquishing ourselves to the Master Lover, the Creator, the Redeemer of all things? If it were that sort of church, Brandon would have every opportunity of meeting Jesus.

Accepting failure and brokenness in each other is simply being honest to what we say we believe about the human condition. To be truly forgiving and restorative is to be honest to what we say about the gospel. If we as the church can learn to express the gospel by helping each other—especially with potentially shameful issues like sexuality—we will demonstrate the sort of love that society desperately needs and will be drawn to.

God's Grace Never Quits on Us

Sometime after I left the wilderness of addictive living, a couple of young people who lived next door asked if I'd do their wedding. I told them yes, then realized I wasn't ordained anymore. The guys in my clergy recovery group thought it was hilarious that I was going to the Internet to find an online ordination. Then one of them mentioned he had his own not-for-profit ministry organization, and he'd ordain me. So on a sunny Saturday afternoon—in the outdoor prayer garden of the church I'd planted over twenty years before—he and one other member of our group met with me to have a quiet, simple ordination service. I had no idea what was about to happen.

Two background pieces are helpful here. When I was a freshman in college, I spent winter break on work crew at a Young Life camp. In the afternoons we had a Bible study, called Campaigners, and after I'd said something one afternoon during our discussion time, our group leader, Chuck, turned to me and said, "Ryan, I'm calling you Rock from now on. Your faith is so solid it reminds me of Peter, and Jesus called him Rock." His affirmation made me feel really good, except even then I had an uneasy sense about myself. Hiddenness, shame and compulsive behavior already had me in their terrifying grip. But I believed the gospel, I really did, and what Chuck thought and said meant a lot to me.

Flash forward almost thirty-five years later to the morning in my study when the Spirit emblazoned on my consciousness that word of Jesus, "Simon, Simon, Satan has asked to sift you as wheat, but I have prayed for you that your faith may not fail. And when you have turned again, strengthen your brothers" (Luke 22:31-32 NIV 1984). Simon is Peter—Rock being Jesus' nickname for him. I paid attention to this, but had no idea what it meant for me.

Now back to the simple, quiet ordination in the prayer garden. One of the guys read the passage from John's Gospel about the night of Jesus' arrest and mock trial, when Peter had declared that he would not leave Jesus no matter what happened or how he was threatened. When the opportunity to stand with Jesus came, Peter buckled and denied knowing him. Three times. Luke's account says that after the third time of denying that he even knew Jesus, Peter went out and "wept bitterly," no doubt awash in feelings of deep remorse and bitter regret. Those are similar to feelings I have experienced over and over and over.

And then, the other began to read John 21:15-17:

When they had finished breakfast, Jesus said to Simon Peter, "Simon, son of John, do you love me more than these?" He said to him, "Yes, Lord; you know that I love you." He said to him, "Feed my lambs." He said to him a second time, "Simon, son of John, do you love me?" He said to him, "Yes, Lord; you know that I love you." He said to him, "Tend my sheep." He said to him the third time, "Simon, son of John, do you love me?" Peter was grieved because he said to him the third time, "Do you love me?" and he said to him, "Lord, you know everything; you know that I love you." Jesus said to him, "Feed my sheep."

They didn't know about the story of when I was on Young Life work crew and Chuck called me Rock. They didn't know about my experience with the Luke 22 passage. This was one of those experiences God delights in arranging to surprise his children and pull them deeper into his grasp of grace. Why the three statements of denial by Peter? Why the three questions of love put by Jesus to Peter? Three in these instances gives the sense of fullness and completion. Peter fully and completely failed. Jesus fully and completely reinstated him.

If you read the whole New Testament, you'll see that Peter did not become the perfect man. He was still capable of getting some really important things wrong. But he belonged to Jesus, and he was secure in his belonging. I'm living free of compulsive behaviors today, a life I never imagined could be mine. I'm not completely reintegrated, not whole yet. I'm making great progress, but that's only because I work my program, use my sponsor, cultivate my daily spiritual connection with God and actively develop mindfulness.

I know my old wiring is still there, and I could relapse, but I work hard to partner with God so that doesn't happen. Even if I did relapse, it wouldn't change who God is. It wouldn't change what he has done. And it wouldn't change who I am to God—it wouldn't change my identity.

Think of Jesus reinstating Peter. When we see Jesus, we see God. He never quits on us, never turns his back. So we should not quit on ourselves. Or each other. For his sake.

Appendix

The group meeting protocol I've developed for a men's compulsive sexual behaviors recovery group at the church I attend is based on the Twelve Steps and my own experience with recovery groups. It is formatted to fit into a distinctly Christian context.

■ ■ ■

Shame No More Group
at Jacob's Well

Now the Lord is the Spirit, and where the Spirit of the Lord is,
there is freedom.
And we all, with unveiled face, beholding the glory of the Lord,
are being transformed into the same image from
one degree of glory to another.
For this comes from the Lord who is the Spirit. . . .
So we do not lose heart. Though our outer self is wasting away,
our inner self is being renewed day by day.
For this light momentary affliction is preparing for us an eternal
weight of glory beyond all comparison,
as we look not to the things that are seen but to the things that are unseen.
For the things that are seen are transient, but the things
that are unseen are eternal.

—2 CORINTHIANS 3:17-18; 4:16-18

Both the one who makes people holy and those who are
made holy are of the same family. So Jesus is not ashamed
to call them brothers and sisters.

—HEBREWS 2:11 TNIV

Welcome

Welcome to this meeting of the Shame No More group at Jacob's
Well.

Purpose of This Ministry

The purpose of the Shame No More group is to help men in the Ja-
cob's Well community who are struggling with compulsive sexual
behaviors to find practical help, spiritual integration and genuine
community, which will result in experiencing and sharing the ho-
listic spiritual freedom Jesus wants all of us to have.

Purpose of Our Meeting Today

The purpose of our meeting today is to encourage each of us to
utilize the aid of the Holy Spirit, the benefits of honest and grace-
based community and the tools of the recovery movement to become
healthy, integrated children of God, living out our God-given sexu-
ality as useful members of the family of Jesus.

Meeting Guidelines

- Requirements for attending are willingness to become honest about our compulsive sexual behaviors and desire to become sober and useful as Jesus defines that for us

- Avoid excessive details

- Exercise care in addressing others and their issues

- Maintain confidentiality and protect the sacred journeys of each other

- What we hear here and who we see here stays here when we leave here

The Signs of Sexual Compulsivity

(from *Don't Call It Love*, Dr. Patrick Carnes, pp. 11-12)
1. A pattern of out-of-control behavior
2. Severe consequences due to sexual behavior
3. Inability to stop despite adverse consequences
4. Persistent pursuit of self-destructive or high-risk behavior
5. Ongoing desire or effort to limit sexual behavior
6. Sexual obsession and fantasy as a primary coping strategy
7. Increasing amounts of sexual experience because the current level of activity is no longer sufficient
8. Severe mood changes around sexual activity
9. Inordinate amounts of time spent in obtaining sex, being sexual or recovering from sexual experience
10. Neglect of important social, occupational or recreational activities because of sexual behavior

The Twelve Steps

Step One
We admitted that we were powerless over our compulsive sexual behavior and that our lives had become unmanageable.
Step Two
Came to believe that a Power greater than ourselves could restore us to sanity.
Step Three
Turned our will and our lives over to the care of God, as we understood God.
Step Four
Made a searching and fearless moral inventory of ourselves.

Step Five
Admitted to God, to ourselves, and to another human being the exact nature of our wrongs.

Step Six
Were entirely ready to have God remove all these defects of character.

Step Seven
Humbly asked God to remove our shortcomings.

Step Eight
Made a list of all persons we had harmed, and became willing to make amends to them all.

Step Nine
Made direct amends to such people wherever possible, except when to do so would injure them or others.

Step Ten
Continued to take personal inventory and when we were wrong promptly admitted it.

Step Eleven
Sought through prayer and meditation to improve our conscious contact with God *as we understood him*, praying only for knowledge of his will for us and the power to carry that out.

Step Twelve
Having had a spiritual awakening as the result of these steps, we tried to carry this message to other addicts, and to practice these principles in all areas of our lives.

Opening Prayer

A period of silence, noting where our thoughts and feelings are, simply becoming aware and present.

Ask the Holy Spirit to settle us, to quiet and focus our hearts, to use this time to help us to follow Jesus, to be open to the Spirit, to trust and love the Father.

The Serenity Prayer

God, grant me serenity
to accept the things I cannot change,
courage to change the things I can,
and wisdom to know the difference;
living one day at a time,
enjoying one moment at a time;
accepting hardship as a pathway to peace;
taking, as Jesus did,
this sinful world as it is,
not as I would have it;
trusting that You will make all things right
if I surrender to Your will;
so that I may be reasonably happy in this life
and supremely happy with You
forever in the next. Amen

Recovery reading

(Prepared by the group leader for each meeting)[1]

Scripture reading

(Prepared by the group leader for each meeting)[2]

Group discussion

(Roughly forty-five minutes, either about the readings or issues guys are dealing with)

The Promises

(from *Alcoholics Anonymous*, pp. 83-84)
If we are painstaking about this phase of our development, we will be amazed before we are halfway through. We are going to know a

new freedom and a new happiness. We will not regret the past nor wish to shut the door on it. We will comprehend the word serenity and we will know peace. No matter how far down the scale we have gone, we will see how our experience can benefit others. That feeling of uselessness and self-pity will disappear. We will lose interest in selfish things and gain interest in our fellows. Self-seeking will slip away. Our whole attitude and outlook upon life will change. Fear of people and of economic insecurity will leave us. We will intuitively know how to handle situations which used to baffle us. We will suddenly realize that God is doing for us what we could not do for ourselves.

Are these extravagant promises? We think not. They are being fulfilled among us—sometimes quickly, sometimes slowly. They will always materialize if we work for them.

The Lord's Prayer

Our Father
Who art in heaven,
Hallowed be thy name.
Thy kingdom come,
Thy will be done, on earth as it is in heaven.
Give us this day, our daily bread, and
Forgive us our trespasses, as we forgive those who trespass
*   against us.*
And lead us not into temptation,
But deliver us from evil.
For Thine is the kingdom and the power and the glory, forever.
Amen.

The Blessing

May the Lord bless you and keep you,
May the Lord make his face to shine upon you,

May the Lord turn his face towards you and grant you peace.
Now and forever. Amen.

*An example of a Scripture reading is as follows:
   Psalm 38:1-8, 21-22

O LORD, rebuke me not in your anger,
      nor discipline me in your wrath!
For your arrows have sunk into me,
      and your hand has come down on me.

There is no soundness in my flesh
      because of your indignation;
there is no health in my bones
      because of my sin.
For my iniquities have gone over my head;
      like a heavy burden, they are too heavy for me.

My wounds stink and fester
      because of my foolishness,
I am utterly bowed down and prostrate;
      all the day I go about mourning.
For my sides are filled with burning,
      and there is no soundness in my flesh.
I am feeble and crushed;
      I groan because of the tumult of my heart. . . .

Do not forsake me, O LORD!
      O my God, be not far from me!
Make haste to help me,
      O Lord, my salvation!

Acknowledgments

Where do I begin to acknowledge those who've made the significant contributions necessary for a journey like mine to unfold? Three men come immediately to mind. Joe Ungashick, dear friend, confidante, you have demonstrated uncommon love and faithfulness and have walked the path few would choose to take. Jim L., my sponsor, I owe you more than I'll ever be able to repay; my recovering is a testimony to God's grace and your selfless giving. Thank you. Mike Boniello, therapist, friend, architect of my psychological restructuring and the "Bishop of well-being," thank you.

John Larsen, my first therapist, you met me with such grace and precisely what I needed and could handle. Thank you for your expertise and your gentleness.

Special thanks to Bill Lytle and Jim L. for painstakingly working through the initial manuscript and offering insights and corrections that have made this a much better book. Special thanks as well to Nancy Lytle for unflagging spiritual and emotional support.

There are those who've helped Pam and me with financial support, great moral encouragement and prayers. You know who you are, and we are very grateful for you. While I can't list everyone who has supported and encouraged us, I would be remiss not to mention Tom and Kari Lipscomb and Tim and

Mary Beth Sotos. Early on, you reached out to us, encouraged us and lifted us. Thank you so much. Troy and Cathy Burns, dear friends and colaborers for many, many years, you have encouraged our hearts more than you know. Kent and Kate Swearingen—what sustained encouragers you have been! Kent, thank you for your encouragement to write. David and Holly Willson, thank you both for your generosity and personal encouragement.

I owe a particular debt of gratitude to Phillip Sandifer for so many points and directions of encouragement. It was Phillip who first said that, because of what God was doing in my life, I should write down my story and offer it as encouragement to others. With his wife, Renee, he has been a sojourner in our small group with Barb and Peter Spokes, dear friends who have made the journey with us.

Jimmy Dodd deserves huge thanks and gratitude from both Pam and me for caring for us so lovingly and for inviting me into an adjunct working relationship with him at PastorServe when I was so weak, beat-up and raw. Jimmy is a gift to those in church leadership, and I count myself fortunate to be his friend.

Pam and I have a mutual friend who has been important to us all our life together, but never more so than in recent years. Brent Bishop has prayed unflaggingly and been a source of God's particular love and care. Thank you, Brent, for being such a good friend.

Thank you to the fellows in my pastors' support group; you've walked with me through some very tough, very dark days. Thank you for sharing the journey; keep going—each of you bears Christ's image in such significant and courageous ways. Thanks as well to my brothers in recovery at Jacob's Well. You are valiant coworkers with me in living out the gospel in our community.

Vivian Baumgartner, you have been an instructor, encourager and bearer of Christ to many, many people over your years of cheerful and heartfelt service to Jesus and his people. Thank you for your generous, maternal love for me and Pam and for your prayers. You are a gift to us.

I am grateful for Brennan Manning and his skillful spiritual direction and specific care to Pam and me during some terribly difficult times. You made the "ragamuffin gospel" come alive for us, Brennan, and we will be grateful forever.

I am particularly thankful for the community of Glenstal Abbey, Murroe, County Limerick, Ireland, for your Christ-centered hospitality and generous spirit. You ministered to me much more than you'll ever imagine. I think of you often, pray for you regularly and miss you terribly. I long to be with you again, and soon.

I am grateful for the community and leadership of Jacob's Well and especially its founders, Tim and Mimi Keel. When Pam and I were at our lowest, you received us just as we were, placed on us neither expectations nor judgments, and gave us a context for grieving, sorting and healing.

And I am most grateful for the role Walt and Thanne Wangerin have played in the life Pam and I have had together. Walt and Thanne, you made such a warm and nurturing contribution to Pam's spiritual and emotional development and well-being, and then you graciously folded me in when I came along. Thank you for your generosity and love. Walt, thank you for such a moving foreword to this book.

Thank you, too, to Dave Zimmerman and the rest of the team at InterVarsity Press. Thank you for extending grace and trust to me, for putting forward the messages of this book, and for helping me communicate these messages with a style and an integrity that I hope will add to the robust contribution IVP has long been making to healthy Christian thought and life.

Every generation stands on the shoulders of the one that has gone before. Each in their own way, my mother's three sisters, Peggy, Dorothy and Barbara, have been sources of comfort and love for me. I still miss my paternal grandmother, Lena Elizabeth Ryan, and her uncommonly steady love, patience and gentleness. My father's sisters, Cathy and Donna, have blessed me throughout my life with consistent love and gentle happiness. I am grateful for each of you.

And to my father-in-law, Nelson Sandefur: you and Sue, gone on before us and too early at that, have been so very good to me. Nelson, your encouragement over the years and particularly your kindness and understanding when Pam and I told you the things you hadn't known about our journey made a difficult conversation an occasion of grace. Lori and Lisa, thank you for your love and acceptance. We are so grateful for each of you.

To my children, Kip, Courtney, Molly and Graham, you are each such wonderfully unique and gifted people. I cannot imagine how difficult it has been for you to deal with aspects of my journey as it has overlapped yours. I am so grateful for the love and acceptance each of you has given me. Being your dad is a privilege that still overwhelms me with fullness of joy and tears.

And Pammie, I write about you in this book, and I refer to you often when I preach and teach; you really are my partner. But the things most dear, that I want you to know . . . these are expressions that belong only to you and me.

Notes

Preface
[1]HealthyMind.com statistics for 2003; see <www.healthymind.com/s-porn-stats>.
[2]Ibid.
[3]Marnie C. Ferree, *No Stones*, 2nd ed. (Downers Grove, Ill.: IVP Books, 2010), p. 71.
[4]HealthyMind.com.
[5]Ferree, *No Stones*, p. 62.
[6]Ibid., p. 63.

Chapter 1: Living a Divided Life
[1]William A. Miller, *Your Golden Shadow* (New York: Harper & Row, 1989), p. 29.
[2]Patrick Carnes, *Out of the Shadows* (Minneapolis: CompCare Publishers, 1983).
[3]Gerald May, *Addiction and Grace* (New York: Harper & Row, 1988), p. 14.
[4]*Alcoholics Anonymous*, 3rd ed. (New York: Alcoholics Anonymous World Services, 1976), p. 39.
[5]Ibid.

Chapter 2: Sexuality and Spirituality
[1]"Statistics and Information on Pornography in the USA," <www.blazinggrace.org/cms/bg/pornstats>.
[2]Mark Patrick Hederman, *Love Impatient, Love Unkind* (New York: Crossroad, 2004), p. 100.
[3]Rob Bell, *Sex God* (Grand Rapids: Zondervan, 2009), p. 42.
[4]N. T. Wright, *Simply Christian* (San Francisco: HarperCollins, 2006), p. x.
[5]Ibid., pp. 33-34.
[6]C. S. Lewis, *The Great Divorce* (San Francisco: HarperOne, 1973), p. 114. This quote comes at the end of a section where Lewis gives a brilliant picture of how the Spirit of God can take what is dim and distorted in our lives and transform it into glowing new life in Christ. Every person who struggles with compulsive sexual behaviors and self-loathing would benefit from reading and rereading this passage.
[7]William M. Struthers, *Wired for Intimacy: How Pornography Hijacks the Male Brain* (Downers Grove, Ill.: InterVarsity Press, 2009), p. 13.

Chapter 3: Coming to Know the Enemy Within
[1]These concepts are from Patrick Carnes, *Out of the Shadows*, 3rd ed. (Center City, Minn.: Hazelden, 2001), pp. 5-15.

[2]William M. Struthers, *Wired for Intimacy: How Pornography Hijacks the Male Brain* (Downers Grove, Ill.: InterVarsity Press, 2009), p. 90.
[3]Ibid., p. 105.

Chapter 4: Shame and "Morality"
[1]Lewis Smedes, *Shame and Grace* (New York: HarperCollins, 1993), p. 32.
[2]Therese Jacobs-Stewart, *Mindfulness and the 12 Steps* (Center City, Minn.: Hazelden, 2010), p. 45.
[3]Ibid., p. 47.
[4]Kenneth Bailey, *Jesus Through Middle Eastern Eyes* (Downers Grove, Ill.: InterVarsity Press, 2008), p. 202.
[5]Ibid., p. 207.

Chapter 5: Excavating Origins
[1]Gerald May, *Addiction and Grace* (New York: Harper & Row, 1988), p. 14.
[2]Ibid.
[3]Dr. Todd Frye and Dr. Todd Bowman, "Sexual Obsessions: Understanding and Working with Those Who Struggle" (seminar, MidAmerica Nazarene University, Olathe, Kansas, June 26-27, 2009). Dr. Frye and Dr. Bowman have done some remarkable work in the area of sexual compulsion.

Chapter 6: Genuine Spiritual Transformation and the Recovery Movement
[1]Dallas Willard, *Renovation of the Heart* (Colorado Springs: NavPress, 2002), p. 39.
[2]The software program I use is from CovenantEyes. Information is available at <www.covenanteyes.com>.
[3]*Alcoholics Anonymous*, 3rd ed. (New York: Alcoholics Anonymous World Services, 1976), p. 62.
[4]This and the following list are adapted from ibid., pp. 55-60.
[5]*Alcoholics Anonymous*, pp. 55, 57.
[6]Ibid., pp. 58-59.
[7]N. T. Wright, *After You Believe* (San Francisco: HarperOne, 2010), p. 159.
[8]Dallas Willard, *The Divine Conspiracy* (San Francisco: HarperSanFrancisco, 1998), p. 346.
[9]The best discussion I've read on spiritual transformation and what the apostle is saying in Romans 12 and other transformation passages is in Wright, *After You Believe*, chap. 5, "Transformed by the Renewal of the Mind."
[10]Ron Martoia, personal correspondence.
[11]"Terry McDonell, Editor, *Sports Illustrated*," interview on *Charlie Rose*, aired November 5, 2010, <http://www.charlierose.com/view/interview/11279>.
[12]Wright, *After You Believe*, p. 144.
[13]Lewis Smedes, *Shame and Grace* (New York: HarperCollins, 1993), p. 77.

Chapter 7: Transformation, Struggle and What I Learned
[1]N. T. Wright, *Simply Christian* (San Francisco: HarperCollins, 2006), pp. 48-49.
[2]Specifically Patrick Carnes's *Out of the Shadows, Don't Call It Love, A Gentle Path Through the Twelve Steps* and *Facing the Shadow*; Mark Laaser's *The Secret Sin: Healing*

the *Wounds of Sexual Addiction* and *The Pornography Trap;* and Craig Nakken's *The Addictive Personality.*

[3]The manual for the national recovery group Sexaholics Anonymous by the same name is one of the best I've read; I believe it is currently out of print. *Hope and Recovery* is the manual for Sexual Compulsives Anonymous; it also is very good. There are at least four national groups working at sex addiction recovery, which unfortunately somewhat diffuses the impact a single organization, like AA, has.

[4]Henri Nouwen, *The Wounded Healer* (New York: Doubleday, 1972), p. xvi.

Chapter 8: In the Darkness, He Is There
[1]Gregory Collins, O.S.B., *The Glenstal Book of Icons* (Dublin: Columba Press, 1989), p. 44.

Chapter 9: God, Brokenness and Life in the Mindful Calm
[1]Matthew McKay, Jeffrey C. Wood and Jeffrey Brantley, *The Dialectical Behavior Therapy Skills Workbook* (Oakland, Calif.: New Harbinger, 2007), p. 63.

[2]In Matthew 6:34, Jesus says, "Therefore do not be anxious about tomorrow, for tomorrow will be anxious for itself. Sufficient for the day is its own trouble." With a slightly different approach, Paul said something similar about focusing on what matters when he wrote to the Philippians, "Finally, brothers, whatever is true, whatever is honorable, whatever is just, whatever is pure, whatever is lovely, whatever is commendable, if there is any excellence, if there is anything worthy of praise, *think about these things*. What you have learned and received and heard and seen in me—*practice these things*, and the God of peace will be with you" (4:8-9, italics added).

[3]Margaret Mary Funk, O.S.B., *Thoughts Matter* (New York: Continuum, 1998), p. 14.

[4]Gerald May, *Addiction and Grace* (New York: Harper & Row, 1988), p. 160.

[5]Ibid.

[6]Therese Jacobs-Stewart, *Mindfulness and the 12 Steps* (Center City, Minn.: Hazelden, 2010), p. 9.

[7]Step twelve: "Having had a spiritual awakening as the result of these steps, we tried to carry this message to other addicts, and to practice these principles in all our affairs."

[8]*Twelve Steps and Twelve Traditions* (New York: Alcoholics Anonymous World Services, 1999), p. 123.

[9]*Alcoholics Anonymous*, 3rd ed. (New York: Alcoholics Anonymous World Services, 1976), p. 124.

[10]Take into account that there's evidence that Samson was a sex addict himself, so the story has all the more meaning for people like me.

[11]Gregory of Nyssa, commentary on 1 Timothy 3:2, in *Colossians, 1-2 Thessalonians, 1-2 Timothy, Titus, Philemon*, ed. Peter Gorday, Ancient Christian Commentary on Scripture (Downers Grove, Ill.: InterVarsity Press, 2000), p. 170.

[12]*Twelve Steps*, pp. 124-25.

Chapter 10: Brokenness and Healthy Spiritual Community
[1]Nate Larkin, *Samson and the Pirate Monks* (Nashville: Thomas Nelson, 2006), p. 54.

[2]Dietrich Bonhoeffer, *Life Together* (New York: Harper & Row, 1954), p. 30.

[3]Larkin, *Samson*, p. 187.

[4]Ibid.

[5]Dr. Todd Frye and Dr. Todd Bowman, "Sexual Obsessions: Understanding and

Working with Those Who Struggle" (seminar, MidAmerica Nazarene University, Olathe, Kansas, June 26-27, 2009).

[6]Margaret Mary Funk, O.S.B., *Thoughts Matter* (New York: Continuum, 1998), p. 21. I find it fascinating that neurological studies have revealed that our food and sex drives are closely linked, originating in the amygdala, the more primal, survival part of the human brain.

Chapter 11: Biblical Ethics and Sexual Behavior

[1]Mark Yarhouse, Richard Butman and Barrett McRay, *Modern Psychopathologies* (Downers Grove, Ill.: InterVarsity Press, 2005), p. 310.

[2]Lewis Smedes, *Sex for Christians*, rev. ed. (Grand Rapids: Eerdmans, 1994), pp. 107-8.

[3]Ibid., p. 110.

Chapter 12: Broken Leaders and Spiritual Rehab

[1]Henri Nouwen, *The Wounded Healer* (New York: Doubleday, 1972), p. 87.

[2]"Statistics and Information on Pornography in the USA," <www.blazinggrace.org/cms/bg/pornstats>.

[3]Nouwen, *Wounded Healer*, pp. 72-73.

[4]We might interpret Paul's words "for the gifts and the calling of God are irrevocable" in a corporate sense (Romans 11:29), but it seems to me that God does not operate with a neat division between corporate and individual application of truth. So in this instance, the gifts and calling God places on an individual remain on that individual, and it is in the church's best interests to help that individual do what is necessary to become healthy and use her gifts and calling for the greater good of the church.

Appendix

[1]A recovery reading might be drawn from the Big Book of Alcoholics Anonymous: for example, for step four—"Made a searching and fearless moral inventory of ourselves"—we might read the section titled "How It Works," in *Alcoholics Anonymous*, 3rd. ed. (New York: Alcoholics Anonymous World Services, 1976), pp. 63-65.

[2]A Scripture reading is related to the recovery reading; in the case of step four, a related Scripture reading might be Psalm 38:1-8, 21-22.

Bibliography

Alcoholics Anonymous [the Big Book]. 3rd ed. New York: Alcoholics Anonymous World Services, 1976.

Bailey, Kenneth. *Jesus Through Middle Eastern Eyes*. Downers Grove, Ill.: InterVarsity Press, 2008.

Banks, Rober, and R. Paul Stevens, eds. *The Complete Book of Everyday Christianity*. Downers Grove, Ill.: InterVarsity Press, 1997.

Bell, Rob. *Sex God*. Grand Rapids: Zondervan, 2007.

Bonhoeffer, Dietrich. *Life Together*. New York: Harper & Row, 1954.

Carnes, Patrick. *Don't Call It Love*. New York: Bantam Books, 1991.

————. *Out of the Shadows*. 3rd ed. Center City, Minn.: Hazelden, 2001.

Ferree, Marnie C. *No Stones: Women Redeemed from Sexual Addiction*. 2nd ed. Downers Grove, Ill.: InterVarsity Press, 2010.

Funk, Margaret Mary, O.S.B. *Thoughts Matter*. New York: Continuum, 1998.

Hart, Archibald. *The Sexual Man*. Nashville: Word Books, 1994.

Hederman, Mark Patrick. *Love Impatient, Love Unkind*. New York: Crossroad, 2004.

Hope and Recovery. Center City, Minn.: Hazelden, 1987.

Jacobs-Stewart, Therese. *Mindfulness and the 12 Steps*. Center City, Minn.: Hazelden, 2010.

Laaser, Mark R. *Healing the Wounds of Sexual Addiction*. Grand Rapids: Zondervan, 2004.

Larkin, Nate. *Samson and the Pirate Monks*. Nashville: Thomas Nelson, 2006.

Lewis, C. S. *The Great Divorce.* San Francisco: HarperOne, 1973.

Manning, Brennan. *Abba's Child.* Colorado Springs: NavPress, 1994.

May, Gerald. *Addiction and Grace.* New York: Harper & Row, 1988.

McKay, Matthew, Jeffrey C. Wood and Jeffrey Brantley. *The Dialectical Behavior Therapy Skills Workbook.* Oakland, Calif.: New Harbinger, 2007.

Miller, William A. *Your Golden Shadow.* New York: Harper & Row, 1989.

Nakken, Craig. *The Addictive Personality.* Center City, Minn.: Hazelden, 1996.

Nouwen, Henri. *The Wounded Healer.* New York: Doubleday, 1979.

Peck, M. Scott. *The Road Less Traveled.* New York: Simon and Schuster, 1978.

Sexaholics Anonymous. Simi Valley, Calif.: SA Literature, 1989.

Smedes, Lewis. *Sex for Christians.* Rev. ed. Grand Rapids: Eerdmans, 1994.

————. *Shame and Grace.* New York: HarperCollins, 1993.

Struthers, William. *Wired for Intimacy: How Pornography Hijacks the Male Brain.* Downers Grove, Ill.: InterVarsity Press, 2009.

Twelve Steps and Twelve Traditions. New York: Alcoholics Anonymous World Services, 1999.

VanVonderen, Jeff, Dale Ryan and Juanita Ryan. *Soul Repair.* Downers Grove, Ill.: InterVarsity Press, 2008.

Willard, Dallas. *The Divine Conspiracy.* San Francisco: HarperSanFrancisco, 1998.

————. *Renovation of the Heart.* Colorado Springs: NavPress, 2002.

Wright, N. T. *After You Believe.* San Francisco: HarperOne, 2010.

————. *Simply Christian.* San Francisco: HarperCollins, 2006.

Yarhouse, Mark, Richard Butman and Barrett McRay. *Modern Psychopathologies.* Downers Grove, Ill.: InterVarsity Press, 2005.